Ireland: The Dawning of the Day

First Published in Ireland in 2012 by
Active I.T. Society
c/o Terenure Enterprise Centre
17 Rathfarnham Road
Terenure
Dublin 6w
info@terenure-enterprise.ie
www.terenure-enterprise.ie

Ireland: The Dawning of the Day
ISBN: 978-0-9570495-0-5

A CIP catalogue record for this book is available from the British
Library.

Book design, layout and typesetting by Patrick Lyons
Creative Writing Tuition, Editing & Compilation by Rick Quinn
Cover Design: Suzanne Moncelet of Izus Design.
Cover Photograph by Roger Kenny
Printed in Denmark by Nørhaven, Viborg

Table of Contents

Memoirs

Short Stories

Poems

Biographies

Preface

It all began in 2010 during Bealtaine, the festival of creativity in older people. The Active IT Society in the Terenure Enterprise decided to participate in the festival with a project in which members were invited to write memories and anecdotes under four headings: Childhood, Love is .., My Working Life and Older and Bolder. These pieces of writing were transferred onto panels with old photos and illustrations attached to encapsulate the theme: Framed! My Life in Pictures. The panels were put on display in exhibitions held in Terenure Library, Ballyroan Library and the Pearse Museum.

At the same time, booklets were made up from these panels. These proved extremely popular and prompted the committee of the Active IT Society to launch a bigger project – to publish a book of writings of members of the society. This would provide an outlet for the creativity of older people, make use of their IT skills and at the same time raise much needed funds for the society. I was involved in the original Bealtaine project, so I was asked to conduct a series of courses in creative writing which were intended to provide material for the book.

The name chosen for our book was IRELAND: THE DAWNING of the DAY borrowed from the old Irish song Fáinne Geal an Lae and used as a refrain by Patrick Kavanagh in his poem, Raglan Road. It also picks up the theme of our wonderful Bealtaine event, Welcome the Dawn, held beside the lake in Terenure College in May of last year..

Most importantly, for many of our members the writing project represented a New Dawn – bravely stepping outside their comfort zone to do something they had always nurtured a desire to do. The start of a new, rewarding pastime they can enjoy for the rest of their lives.

Apart from our own writers – talented albeit as yet undiscovered – we decided to invite other individuals who are better known to contribute some pieces of writing to help raise the profile of our publication. A bit of good old-fashioned networking went into action.

A few years ago I spent some time in Mountjoy Prison! No, not for obvious reasons. I had gone there to interview John Lonergan, Governor of the prison at the time, on behalf of the Aware magazine of which I was the editor. Recently, I thought of him as a possible person to write for our book and emailed him. He replied immediately that he would be delighted. His story about how prisoners had built St Brigid's Resource Centre in Killester prompted me to invite some of the creative writers in the centre to submit some of their writings – I had conducted classes there in the past and their ability was well known to me. In a 'Hands across the City' gesture to their fellow writers in Terenure, they agreed to join them in this venture, so we extend a welcome to Pauline O'Regan, Mary Butler and Kay Adams.

Aidan O'Hara, an old friend and neighbour of mine, was another who readily agreed to contribute. A well known writer and broadcaster, he recalls his childhood in Donegal.

Paddy Conneff and I are both past pupils of Synge Street School, as is international singer, John MacNally. I emailed John in Australia to ask him for a piece. He too was delighted to oblige and Paddy and I met John and his brother Donal in Dublin when John was home on holidays during the summer. He even sang 'Mary in the Morning' for me, sitting in the back of my car!

Kevin Conneff of Chieftains fame is Paddy's brother and through Paddy we managed to persuade Kevin to write for us. Kevin is a very busy and much travelled man but he managed to find time for us. The result is a lovely, revealing piece.

Ian O'Doherty, who writes for the Irish Independent' and is well known on TV, was contacted by Ann Moriarty of the Terenure Enterprise Centre and kindly provided a wry take on older people surfing on the Internet. His father-in-law, Sean Gallagher, relates his experience of coming to the world of IT later in life.

Brian Breathnach, artist and writer, was one of the few people to be granted an interview by Samuel Beckett. A friend of mine, I asked him to shares his story of his meeting with Beckett in Paris and he readily agreed.

This book is not like a novel to be read from cover to cover. Keep it on your bedside locker or on your coffee table and dip into it from time to time. You are bound to discover a nugget or two.

ENJOY!

Memoirs

Older & Bolder

Edie Wynne – Deputy Lord Mayor of Dublin, 2010-2011

Mark Twain said: 'Age is an issue of mind over matter. If you don't mind, it don't matter.' I agree! My life has absolutely got more exciting over time.

I grew up in Clones, one of six siblings. As a youngster I was fairly resourceful. I remember arranging crossings, on the henhouse door, of the river at the end of our garden, which was the Border between the Republic and the North of Ireland! I moved to Dublin, where I worked in the Guinness Brewery. Around this time I met my husband, Sean Connery look-a-like Tom Wynne, at a party in Grosvenor Square, Rathmines. Tom has been the rock that has allowed me to achieve my ambitions. We have two daughters – Adrienne and Caroline – who both inherited their mother's adventurous spirit and continue to keep us on our toes.

I went back to study and became a Trinity graduate. I also started to play a more active role in my other passions – politics and community. I got involved in Fine Gael during the Dr. Garret FitzGerald years and have worn out much shoe leather, political campaigning. I also contributed to many local community projects such as the Terenure Enterprise Centre.

I was co-opted as a Dublin City Councillor in October 2007. Then in 2009 my grandchildren got great fun out of seeing Granny's posters up during the local elections which led to my election in my own right as a Dublin City Councillor. The political cherry on the cake was becoming Deputy Lord Mayor in June 2010.

Lord Mayor's Coach

When I travelled from the Mansion House to open the Fáilte Ireland 2010 Dublin Horse Show in the RDS in the Lord Mayor's wonderful horse drawn carriage it was a long way from the little girl crossing the Border river on the henhouse door in Clones. My days are very busy, but I'm loving it and my family are so proud. I hope there's loads more to come.

Like a good wine, my life keeps getting better with time.

Edie Wynne - Deputy Lord Mayor Of Dublin

J'member

Mike Mahon's Confirmation Day

J'member the days we played ball on the streets,
Not a care in the world as we munched on our sweets.
No cars to disrupt us 'cept cops on the beat,
Plodding their way on oversized feet.

J'member the days when the milk was delivered,
The coalman came too in case we were shivered.
A horse pulled the bread van and lots of cake too.
Oh, the smell was divine as we joined in the queue.

J'member the summers when the days were so hot,
It melted the tar as we stood on the spot.
J'member the winters all buried in snow,
When off to the pictures we would all go.

J'member the school where we went to be learning,
T'was a bit of a joke till exam time was looming.
We chewed on our pencils and splattered the ink
As we scratched our gray matter to help us to think.

J'member the mother so kind and so dear,
As she slaved in the kitchen to bring us good cheer.
And dad as he worked in the factory by day,
Arriving back home with plenty of pay.

J'member the days when the feel of a breast,
Would send us off scurrying quick to confess,
To the men in black boxes that lurked in their lair
And left us in tears and utter despair.

Mike Mahon

Push The Boat Out

I was reared on a farm in Curcreigh, Clooneyquinn, County Roscommon. Looking from our farmhouse, we could see Lough Patrick - a picturesque lake with two Islands, plentiful with fish and wild life. My elderly neighbour was a lovely man. His name was Morris Keane. He would go fishing when he finished work on the farm. I would be waiting for him. I was eight years old at the time and he would take me with him. We would circle the lake for some hours in a small flat bottom rowing boat, mostly with good results. Morris supplied me with fishing tackle and taught me how to fish.

At that time the lake and streams joining other lakes were teaming with fish. Mostly we caught pike, perch and eel. I don't remember catching trout. I don't think they were plentiful then. A lovely summer's evening, the sun setting in the west. A nice fresh breeze in your face and the peace and beauty of the countryside. Looking north you could see our house, Conroy's, Breslin's, Carroll's, King's, Connor's and Healy's. Looking south you could see Croghan's, Mannion's and Murray's.

Morris, a bachelor, spent most of his life at sea. He always encouraged me to see the world. I'm afraid I did not take his advice, as I never left Ireland to earn a living. After some hours on the lake I would say to Morris that I wanted to go to the toilet. The answer he would give me, 'Sure there's plenty of room out there; if we don't catch them we will poison them.' So I was first to pollute Lough Patrick.

All of this took place over sixty years ago, but I remember it with great fondness, if not a little sadness. The wild and rugged west was a great place to grow up. The wonderful joy of the wide open spaces and the freedom to play, explore and learn. My boat is heading home now. I can see the promised land in the distance.

It's getting closer by the day.
When that day comes, Morris and I will have a good chat about
the ones that got away.

Kevin McGrath

Too Many Kittens

'Show your friend the kittens.'

I was visiting a house in the country and meeting new people. The grown-ups congregated together and the children were allowed to go away to play in the garden. I was not yet four years old but I went along happily with my companion who was a little older. We went off together to see the kittens.

'There are too many kittens,' my little hostess remarked. 'We'll just be keeping two.' 'What's going to happen to the others?' I enquired. 'Oh! They'll just be drowned.' 'Couldn't we drown them now?' I wondered. We were standing at the side of the house by the rain barrel. 'Let's,' the other girl said.

We climbed up onto the plinth but found that the barrel was covered with a round wooden lid. We prised up the lid and pushed it to one side. We gathered up the tiny kittens, whose eyes were still shut, and helped each other drop them into the water. They swam around in a frenzy and tried to scramble out over the sides, their little claws sticking out desperately trying to catch the rim and cling on. 'They are going to climb out,' we called in unison. 'We'll have to put the lid back on.'

We could hear the little kittens scratching away at the underside of the lid. Obviously they weren't enjoying this drowning business and neither were we. 'We'll have to take them out again,' we shouted.

We managed to push off the lid, and we reached in over the edge of the barrel, lying on the sharp rim and leaning out towards the middle, between us we managed to lift the wet, bedraggled morsels of life out to safety.

With that, the grown-ups arrived, probably realising there

was too much silence about. My aunt had an apprehensive, querying look on her face. 'What are you doing?' 'You shouldn't do such a thing,' she gasped. 'It's alright,' I said. 'We've taken them all out.'
Only now, do I realise what her horrified expression really meant.

Opal Peard

My Life

John MacNally

I grew up in Terenure on the Fortfield Road, went to the Presentation Convent, then to the boys' school beside St Joseph's Church in Terenure, then to the Redemptorists in Limerick. (They thought I might study for the priesthood but, alas, the best laid schemes of mice and men . . .) Then to Coláiste Mhuire, then to the Marist Brothers, and at last to the place where a large amount of Dubs end up – 'Synger'!! – where I was coaxed through the Leaving Cert by a great group of dedicated teachers, whom I fondly remember as Bisto, Tweedy, Ghandi, Jiggers, The Guck, Gilroy and others.

My singing career started in Dublin as a boy soprano with my brother Donal, who at that time was a far better singer than I and was acclaimed in the American newspapers as the best boy soprano in the world of his time. I sang in at many Feis competitions and was brought to all of these by my beloved mother. On one occasion, on the morning of the Feis Matthew, my mother washed my short trousers and asked me to dry them in front of the electric fire. While doing so, dreaming about other things, I burnt a hole in the right leg of the trousers in the front.
Naturally, of course, I said nothing to my mother. When it came

to my turn to sing, I walked on stage with quite a large hole in my pants - which had resulted from some vigourous rubbing to get rid of the burn – with the burn marks around it. My poor mother nearly had a stroke on the spot. At that point, I knew I had to win the Feis to prevent my mother from committing murder!! Luckily, I did win.

When my voice broke, my adult voice started almost immediately. My brother was not so lucky, as nothing returned after his boyhood soprano voice left him.

I have never stopped singing and, thank God, I have had and am still enjoying a wonderfully rewarding career, which has brought me from Ireland to England, to Europe, to America, to Japan, Singapore and, of course, to Australia, where I now live with my wife Anne, our daughter Elizabeth (who has blessed us with three grandsons), and our son Austin.

John MacNally

A Lost Love

Maureen & Bernard

Visitors, father and son, came unexpectedly and introduced themselves, Thomas and Bernard. Their English accent was very pleasant. They were staying for a few days, looking up family relatives. We had a family wedding arranged in Mullingar and they were invited. At the evening dance we met up again and the son, Bernard drove me home. After ten days of his holiday, he proposed to me. I was taken completely by surprise. I would have to go and live in England. That was also a shock.

Sailing from Dún Laoghaire with promises of phone calls and letters, the flowers started coming almost every week. My landlady was puzzled by all the attention. Then a former boyfriend from Donegal came visiting. He saw the bouquets of flowers and said: "I should have expected it". I let him go! Bernard came over for me and we sailed for England. I had made a sort-of bargain with him. I would give him his answer on the anniversary of the day I arrived in England with him. We had a wonderful time – he took me everywhere. He worshipped the ground I walked on.

Sad to say, I watched him die in hospital with the Asian Flu.

It was the exact day I was to have given him my answer to his proposal.

A part of my life died with him that day ....

Maureen Maloney

The Girls At The Weir

Orwell Weir

T he first distraction was vertical. Straight down over my head spilled the contents of a tea pot - tea leaves and all - not yet cold. The old woman, in the little house on the weir, was accustomed to using the river for her trash. 'Lucky me,' I shouted up at her. 'I suppose it could have been your other pot, another time. Don't you know you cannot pollute the river like that?' But, she was deaf, and just shuffled out of view. I was fifteen years old, and was fly-fishing for trout in the pool below the waterfall on the Dodder River at Orwell.

Moving over to the other side of the stream, I commenced casting again. Then, there came a further distraction. Two St. Louis secondary girls with bicycles were peering over the wall at me. Well now, watching girls was another pastime of my age. But, at that moment, I was irritated by the attention. Here was I trying to be a hunter. I was being so stealthy, I imagined that I was as inconspicuous to the fish as a bush. Yet all my precautions might be in vain, as the shadows cast from on high by these lassies could spook the quarry. 'Get away from there,' I screamed. But it was only quietly - In my head sort of. For really, I was far too shy to speak to females of my own age. Just then the rod jerked in my hand, and I was stuck into a cartwheeling fish. Gold coloured with black and red spots, it was easily the biggest fish I had ever hooked.

But my eye had been half on the girls. So, I felt uneasily that my connection with the trout might not be so secure.

The fight went on and on, as the fish careered around, leaping and splashing. Although still on edge, I was gathering confidence and the showman in me was taking over. Glancing up from the parabolic curve of the rod, I made sure that the girls were still watching. Then tragedy! With my eye off the water, the leader snagged against a submerged branch and snapped. In dead silence, the ripples circled and spread and then disappeared. The great fish was gone, already just a memory. The hissing sound of the water returned, as my legs trembled uncontrollably.

After a while, I glanced towards the parapet and saw that the girls were laughing! How could they? 'You silly twits,' I wanted to shout. But as before, no sound came out. After a little while, and in great disappointment, I flopped down on the grassy bank and commenced a week of hating women.

Paddy Conneff

Woodworm

It seemed to me as a small child in Dublin that parents were perfect people who spent most of their lives trying to bring up their children to be perfect like themselves. Fathers went off to work each day to do important things that we couldn't understand. Mothers stayed home and organised the household and the children's lives.

One of the biggest events in our family occurred when mother discovered woodworm in a dressing table in the girls' bedroom. The problem with woodworm, Mother said, was that if it wasn't sorted as soon as possible, it would spread very fast, possibly into the rafters and in no time at all bring the house down around our heads. Dad consulted the chaps in the office who gave him a fail-safe remedy. Mother was dispatched to the hardware store with a list. Paraffin and methylated spirits were mentioned and some chalky stuff to bind it all into a paste. Saturday was given over to the job in hand. The offending piece of furniture was carefully taken down the stairs- making sure not to touch the walls - and out into the back garden. Dad pasted and rubbed for the best part of the morning. Everything progressed nicely and it was decided to let things dry out while we had lunch.

'A quick lick of paint now and the job is done,' Dad said when we resumed in the afternoon. True to his word it really did look great and we stood back to admire. Satisfied with his handiwork, he lit up a cigarette. Flicking away the match, he stood back to have a last look. There was the loudest explosion we had ever heard. The dressing table in burst into flames, the biggest, highest and best bonfire we had ever seen in all our born days!!

Fia Weber

15

My Village

In my village in the Midlands there were four pubs. They did a great trade on weekends and fair days. The fair days were held once a month. All the farmers came with sheep and cattle.. They lined the sheep and cattle up in stalls all along the street. The jobbers came to bargain with the farmers and when a price was agreed there was a handshake to seal the deal. The jobber paid the farmer and the farmer gave a few shillings back to the jobber for luck. This was called the 'luck penny'. When the cattle were sold, the farmers retired to the pub and the wives called in for the money to do the shopping. The wives went home and let the farmers get on with the drinking.

In the summer a carnival came to my village for two weeks. We had a great time at the bumper cars, swinging boats, chair planes, roulette tables and bingo. There were dances for the grown ups every night. All the big bands came, Joe Dolan and the Drifters, Big Tom and the Mainliners, Eileen Reid and the Cadets, Dickie Rock and his band. When Brendan Boyer and the Royal Showband came, everyone did the Huckle Buck. The rest of the year for entertainment, we went to the pictures. The films were always breaking down and when the lights came on, we were all caught kissing in the back row which was a mortal sin at the time.

In June we had the Corpus Christie procession. We were dressed in our best clothes and marched for about four miles, saying the rosary as we walked. Along the route the houses were freshly painted for the occasion. On our return there was Benediction held outside the church.

At Christmas we sold the geese and turkeys to buy the Christmas shopping. On Christmas morning we got up at the crack of dawn to open our presents, and there was great excitement.

On Stephen's Day, we dressed up in old clothes and painted our faces to hunt the wren and made plenty of money for the pictures that night.

Jim Browne

Memories of Childhood

Bull-Nosed Morris Cowley

My first memory of childhood was when I was about five years old. I was born in Ranelagh, close to Rathmines Townhall, so that we could hear the chimes. We were a large family, eight in all. I was the youngest of three boys. We were fairly well off. We had a housemaid and I used to think we also had a nurse. Well, with my mother having eight children in the space of twelve years, all born at home, and with the midwife was so often in the house, I might be forgiven for thinking that.

We also had a motor car, the only one on the street. It was a bull-nosed Morris Cowley, open topped, and quite large. It would have to be with such a large family. It was our custom for my father to take the family out for a drive on Sunday afternoon. On this occasion in the month of February, we were going to the Pine Forest to see the snow, which was visible from our house. Fully loaded as we were, this put a great strain on the engine. As we got near to the snow line, a great billow of smoke came from the engine. My father stopped quickly ordered everybody out of the car. He then lifted the bonnet to find a small flame just starting. With great presence of mind he ran to the side of the road, scooped up hands-full of snow and dumped them on the engine, putting out the fire.

It was discovered that an inner tube had fallen from the tool-box above the engine. It had melted and caught fire. However, quick thinking by my father had saved the day and we were soon able to continue our journey. What an exciting afternoon.

Albert Connor

My Sporting Life

The Race Is On!

My earliest memory of sport was a dreary wet Sunday at home and Michael O'Hehir, commentating on Gaelic football or hurling. In those days we had no telly, so unless you went to a match it was very boring. In the summer I would go down to my cousin in Clontarf and she would bring me to Clontarf Baths for a swim. She was a member of Clontarf Ladies Swimming Club and I joined the following year.

I remember Clontarf was divided in two - the bigger side for the boys and the other side for the girls. The wall was soon demolished some years later. There were some very good swimmers but I wasn't one of them. In full tide the better swimmers would swim out to the bollard in the bay. Tuesday was our Club Night. There was no comparison to the training the swimmers do today. It was mostly natural talent. We had some good times there and got invited to all the parties. It was at Joan Green's party that I met my future husband. It was inevitable that our children would be swimmers. In fact my eldest son was a great swimmer and qualified for the Olympic Games in Montreal, 1976 and four years later in Moscow.

I still love to swim but in the 1967, I joined Newland's Golf

Club and it's there that I found my favourite sport.
I still play and can give my grandchildren a good match.

Eileen Williamson

A Visit To The Guinness Storehouse In Dublin

Henry family enjoying the 'Black Stuff'

O n 13th April 2011 some eleven members of the Active IT Society made the trip, led by Mrs. Angela Hickey. The Storehouse can be envisaged as a museum of the Guinness Brewery, in successful production of 'porter' beer since 1759 at Dublin's St. James's Gate.

We started at the usual point, namely the entrance to 'Guinness Storehouse' about 11.00 am, and bought our €9 tickets, which included the cost of a pint of draft Guinness stout in the 'Gravity Bar' on the seventh floor right at the top of the building. A vast amount of technical information is available about the brewing process for those interested, as one follows the guiding arrows along the intended trip, and listens to video instructions.

We learnt that clean water is brought from sources in County Wicklow. During each year some 100,000 tonnes of Irish malting barley is used as one main ingredient, as well as some imported barley. Some 3 million pints of beer are produced each day, for home sale and export. The barley is first soaked for a couple of days, until it begins to sprout. It is then dried and roasted and ground up, being "malt" at this stage. It is now mixed with hot water and mashed, and the liquid (called 'wort') drained off. The solid residue becomes animal feed. The wort is next boiled for 70 minutes with chopped hop-cones (imported), to give the bitter characteristic flavour. Next, yeast is added, to ferment the wort and produce some 7 percent alcohol content, during a two-day period. The yeast is then removed, and the remaining liquid is porter of an amber colour, needing some further maturing etc. before packing in casks for sale. The removed yeast is usable in further fermentation runs, with some of the yeast being sold for baking bread and other uses. This whole brewing process is shown in detail, step by step, with video commentary.

After the tour we ascended to the Gravity Bar, to enjoy our pints - we had already sampled a small measure, to indicate the taste, when we reached the end of the production process demonstration. A panoramic view of Dublin and environs is available through the windows of the circular wall surrounding this Bar. To the west one can see the Wellington Monument of Phoenix Park; to the south one sees the Dublin hills, to the east Howth Head and lighthouse, and to the north Croke Park.

A leisurely lunch in the fifth-floor restaurant followed, at very reasonable prices, with coffee or tea on the house. All in all, this visit has provided a memorable and very enjoyable experience.

Eamon Henry

Willie Bermingham

Willie Bermingham Place

W hen Willie Bermingham was young, working with the Dublin Fire Brigade in 1977, he found an old man lying dead in appalling circumstances in a timber chalet in Charlemont Street. It was cold and there was no food or fuel in the place. The old man was stiff in death, alone and miserable. Willie encountered many such cases in his time with the Dublin Fire Brigade. These conditions of isolation and despair prompted him and his friends to launch a campaign to raise awareness of the living conditions of the forgotten older people of the capital city.

ALONE was founded by Willie Bermingham in 1977 and for thirteen years, he was the main man. He died at the age of 48. In death his name is still synonymous with the organisation. In 1979 Willie received an Irish People of the Year award and in 1985 he received the International Fire Fighter of the Year accolade. In 1988 he received an Honorary Doctorate of Law from Trinity College, Dublin.

I met Willie Bermingham only twice. The first time was when he appointed me to be his quantity surveyor on the new building complex of 20 units that he was then planning for Kilmainham Lane. The second time was when he turned the sod for the project in April 1990. After the ceremony, I went with him to a pub in James Street for a pint of Guinness. With us were Pat O' Brien, architect and Liam Ó Cuanaigh, one of Willie's associates.

Willie's health was not good and he appeared frail. He walked me out of the pub into the street, both of us with pint glasses in hand. He moved backwards towards the kerb of the wide footpath opposite St. James Hospital.

I was concerned that he would fall on to the road, which was busy with traffic. By then I realised that he was looking upwards at the first floor wall over the pub. 'Did you know that Willie Cosgrave was born and lived here?' he said as he pointed. Sure enough there was a plaque on the wall of No.174, commemorating the former Taoiseach. A week after this event, Willie Bermingham died. I knew that when he had cut the sod at Kilmainham he was suffering from cancer, and that he had by then suffered three heart attacks. The fourth one killed him.

Willie's funeral was memorable. Instead of a hearse, his coffin was transported on a Dublin Fire Brigade tender with his workmates forming a guard of honour. A Catholic private Mass was celebrated in his house in Inchicore by a local priest. This was in deference to his religious roots. His remains were then taken to St. Patrick's Cathedral for the public ceremony. Willie had made all of the arrangements himself. He had been very impressed by the support received from the Dean of St. Patrick's for his work with the poor and ALONE. An abiding memory of the ceremony in the Cathedral was the acoustics of the great stone building. The singing sounded magnificent.

When the housing project at Kilmainham Lane was complete, the official opening was performed by the new President of Ireland, Dr. Mary Robinson. There were other dignitaries there too. But the main stars at the party were the people Willie had rescued from loneliness and poverty and who were now living in modest comfort in the new complex. That was in 1992. On that occasion Willie was remembered.

The little group of houses has since been named Willie Bermingham Place. A stone monument stands just inside the entrance. It commemorates Willie Bermingham and his great achievement in having the project completed even after his death. The names of his architect, quantity surveyor and engineer are engraved on the stone under his own name and that of his friend, Liam Ó Chuanaigh.

Willie Bermingham is the most unforgettable person I have ever met.

Ar dheis Dé go raibh a anam dílis.

Paddy Conneff

Happy Memories

O'Hara family and friends in Muff in 1946.
Aidan O'Hara is in centre front with his twin brother, Mel (in matching outfit)
to his right on Leo Brennan's knee. Leo is father of the Clannad family.

My memories of life in Muff, County Donegal, in the 1940s are almost entirely happy and positive ones, and Kilderry Wood – known as 'the Plantin' - nearby on the shores of Lough Foyle was our playground, where we were Finn Mc-Cool and the Fianna, one day, Robin Hood and his Merry Men the next, and Cowboys and Indians a lot of the time. It was a magic place.

I remember the excitement of the annual sports day, and when the circus came to Muff. It was Duffy's Circus, I think, or was it Fossett's? On one occasion a juggler asked me to come into the ring to do something or other and I was mortified because my pants were loose and kept falling down. Laugh? I nearly died! I recall films being shown in the hall across the street from our house, or in tents a couple of times.

I remember the time in the late '40s when the Harding Family travelling show came to Muff, performing in the hall, and staying several days. One of them was a handsome young man called Leo, and I think all the older girls, including my sisters, might have fancied him. Anyway, when it came time for the Hardings to leave I wanted to go with them, and Leo told me to go home and get my trousers pressed. He probably wanted to get rid of this pesky kid. I had never heard that word 'pressed' used in that way because our clothes were always ironed. When I told my mother, I was quickly disabused of the notion and the Hardings left without me. But that young man, Leo, was none other than Leo Brennan who went on to gain fame throughout Donegal as the singer and accordion player with the Slieve Foy Showband, and later as father of the Brennans of the internationally renowned group, Clannad – Enya, Moya, Ciarán and Paul.

I have many more happy memories of when I was a boy in Muff in the 1940s. My father was transferred to the Garda station in Buncrana on the Lough Swilly side of the Inishowen peninsula in February 1949 and that's when we left. But the memories of Muff are still vivid and full of bliss.

Aidan O' Hara

A Strong Memory.....

Maureen Maloney

My Mother rarely ever complained about being ill, so it was a little disconcerting to hear her say, when I asked her how she was feeling the night before she died: 'Fair,' she said, 'Fair.'

After I retired that night I had a dream – that my Mother was dead. I awoke next morning in a terrible state. I rushed down to her bedroom. My Mother was indeed dead. She had died in her sleep. The awful thing about it all was that for some time afterwards I thought I was still in the dream but reality soon steeped in.

I deeply mourn her quiet passing to this day.

Maureen Maloney

The Sweep

Irish Hospital Sweepstakes' Draw

Transition years hadn't been invented then but due to a stan-doff with Mother over the selection of a school for Leaving Cert, I applied for and got a job with Irish Hospitals Sweepstakes in Ballsbridge. Commonly known as 'The Sweep,' it really was a unique place to work. There were a number of draws each year based on The Classics in the English racing calendar.

By far the largest number of sweepstake tickets were sold in America, and this was done through agents living out there, totally illegal as it transpired. Probably because of this, every ticket sold was receipted separately. About one thousand women were employed on a part-time basis to facilitate this. The period of employment lasted between six and eight weeks at a time, and included overtime and Saturday and Sunday work at the end of the term. It was boring work, but the canteen provided beautiful food of an extremely high quality and this, combined with regu-lar breaks and truly great pay rates, made it very acceptable. The building was a great barn of a place with a central aisle that ran from the posh front offices down to the canteen at the rear. On either side the most rudimentary dividers separated the space into large sections.

The work force was remarkable in itself. At a time when women were expected to retire from paid work on marriage, there was a high proportion of older women, many widows and a large smattering of out of work actors, dancers and artists. This led to an interesting mix at the large wooden tables where about ten women sat. I was assigned to the Irish section, but we also dealt with the overflow from the American section. There were probably about forty of these tables in our part of the building. It resembled a conveyor belt in the fact that the tickets passed through a number of processes before finally going into the first set of drums.   Security was strict and everyone very conscious of their part in the process. If a mistake was picked up by a member of staff, it could mean a reward of an eight week stint at the following draw.

The millions of tickets eventually went into large drums. A certain percentage were drawn out of these and placed in the iconic drums we saw in the ads with the tickets being drawn by nurses in uniform. The number of horses in the race predicated the number of drums and a final ticket was drawn from each of these to correspond to each of the runners. The winning horse was obviously the winning ticket.

I stayed working for three or four sweeps but common sense prevailed, and I returned to full time education, my grasp of world geography greatly enhanced by my experience.

Fia Weber

The Antique Wall Clock

Antique Wall Clock

I was born in Rathroe, Mantua, Co. Roscommon and was the youngest of eight children. My mother died when I was 1 year and 8 months old. My Aunt Celia and Uncle Pat were wonderfully kind people. They took me into their home and reared me as one of their own family. They had one boy and two girls. Their home was also a thatched farmhouse about five miles South East from my home in Curcreagh, Clooneyquinn, County Roscommon.

When we were very young, M.J. and I slept in the kitchen in a settle bed. It was a double bed at night and folded in the daytime into a piece of furniture. At the bottom of our large kitchen was the bedroom, where just inside the door you would find the Antique Wall Clock hanging.

It chimed the hour and half hour bell and had a very distinctive tick. When the fire was raked at night and the oil lamp put out, our kitchen was pitch dark, as was the bedroom and the parlour. When I was young, I often woke up during the night and would be frightened at first. However, as soon as I heard the clock ticking, it had a calming affect on me and I would not be afraid anymore. My Aunt Celia and Uncle Pat had two daughters Annie and Úna and they slept in the bedroom.

The clock was wound once a week and that was Uncle Pat's job. As well as telling the time and having a calming affect on me, the clock had one other very important function. It acted as a safe for Uncle Pat. When he came home from a fair after selling cattle, he would put the bundle of money under the pendulum in the well of the clock. That is where the money was kept.

The only entrance to the house was by the kitchen door. It had a latch on the outside that you lifted and walked in.
It was the custom for neighbours to walk into the kitchen and they would be made most welcome. I don't remember the door ever being locked day or night. I have no knowledge of our house or any neighbour's house being robbed.

I have a fascination with clocks to this day. At one time, I restored marble mantle clocks. My good wife Eileen would throw them in the dustbin if she had her way. The reason was I worked on them at night. My workbench was our kitchen table and I'm afraid to admit I did not clean up very well after I finished working there.

That's what upset Eileen and that put an end to my profitable business. The clocks had to go or I had to go.

Kevin McGrath

Christmas Eve When I Was Young

Pauline's Holy Communion Day

A s a child in our house, one of the main exciting events of
the year for me was the annual Christmas Eve Family Supper. All day long, tension mounted as preparations and planning gathered momentum and the annual rituals were performed. By six o'clock in the evening, we children had reached fever-pitch. I, being the youngest of seven siblings knew the drill.....I and my sister who was next in age were dispatched to bed very early after a light supper, with the solemn promise that we would be woken up and brought downstairs when the party began. However, the actual time when the family would finally gather around the big table in the dining room was quite flexible and depended on when the last stragglers in the family bar could be encouraged to go home. Earlier on, one of my brothers would be dispatched to Ballinasloe train station to pick up our older sister who, we all hoped, managed to get on the last train from Dublin after her day's work, while another brother's task was to drive the bar staff home, each one clutching a bottle of Gold Label whiskey, marking my mother's appreciation of their hard work and loyalty.
Finally, the glasses were all washed, the shutters were pulled down and we could relax.

The menu usually included my mother's wholesome soup, followed by roast duck from our grandmother's farm with all of the trimmings and then a large helping of jelly and trifle, all washed down with lots of lemonade for the younger people and something stronger for the older folk. The meal would finish well past midnight when I was ushered back to bed with warnings to get to sleep immediately or Santa Claus may not visit. I was always happy to obey.

Pauline Doyle

Our First Dog

O ur first dog was called Biffo. He was a noble, elegant, blonde Great Dane. When my first born Kevin was a baby, Biffo guarded the pram and when he awoke he alerted me. As the children got older they rode him around the garden. He died suddenly when he was seven years and I was devastated and vowed never to have another dog.

Some years later I was recovering from a 'flu and my husband said he would take the children out for a drive. A few hours later I woke up to a lot of noise on the stairs and suddenly the bedroom door burst open and all four arrived with big smiles on their faces and placed a ball of fluff on top of me. It was a Norwegian Elk Hound puppy. He had the cutest little face and a fluffy white tail that curled over his back. My annoyance soon vanished and very soon he took over the whole family. He was given the name of Biffo No. 2.

All the relations and neighbours called to see this wonder. He had a big personality and everyone loved him. We had a big back garden and he loved to play with all the children of the neighbourhood, but very soon he copped on to climbing the apple tree at the end of the garden, a little jump on to the wall and down into the field at the other side. He loved to play with a little black dog called Blackie, and then he would arrive home via the front door and give a loud bark to get in.

He was discovered sitting up at the shops on Ann Devlin Road waiting for the Bread Man who gave him some stale cakes. Other times, he was known to arrive at Terenure College at break time and follow all the boys who had crisps. They thought he was a wolf and would drop their crisps which he would eat with relish. He was also known to go into the neighbour's side passage and eat the food belonging to Lulu the cat. As I was unaware of all this activity at the time I became worried as he was not eating his food. I brought him to Manfred the vet and he said he had a weight problem and would have to go on a diet. Heads of cabbage and Bovril. Nothing else.

Then one day, Biffo was missing. A whole week went by and no sign of him. The phone rang one night and a very nice lady told us she had found him in her front garden. She thought it was an old coat but on inspection she discovered his identity medal and our phone no. When we collected him there was celebration and jubilation that Biffo was home again.

Many years later when Biffo No. 2 went to the dog's heaven, I was talking to a woman in the locality. The subject of dogs came up. She told me about her wonderful little Blackie. She said she had a litter of beautiful little fluffy pups. As I said goodbye, I wondered had those little black puppies got white fluffy tails!

Eileen Williamson

'The Fish Lady'

Phena O'Boyle

Maybe I was lucky, as I choose to work with food for most of my life and it was for me a past-time and a passion. In 1969, I joined the marketing division of the Irish Sea Fisheries Board, otherwise known as BIM.

For the next 27 years, (with a two year break with Concern Worldwide), it took over my life. I checked fish landings around Ireland, and prices at the fish markets. On four mornings a week, I told the fishermen and the nation all about the sea and seafood on RTE radio. I became known as 'The Fish Lady'.

With missionary zeal I tempted Irish people to eat this great food. I even had ideas to turn Ireland into a 'Seafood Island' and its twenty eight inhabited islands into 'Seafood Islands' too! To make my point I opened The Periwinkle Seafood Bar in 1982, serving only fish of course.

My colleagues and I filleted mackerel, gutted herrings, opened oysters, dreamt up wonderful recipes, photographed delicious dishes for advertising, recipe books and our annual BIM calendar. We gave demonstrations and courses around Ireland

and promoted seafood in Europe and the U S. Some of my best memories are of the courses I gave on our islands off the west coast.

On Inishfree Island, off Burtonport in Donegal, I gave a one-day course in 1986. There was no electricity. So by the light of candles and a big turf fire in the living room there was poetry, song and stories, as we planned our course for next day. We cooked up chowders, stews and salads, enjoyed them and then all joined in dance and song before leaving for Belfast and Donegal on the last and only boat for the mainland.

My working life – mostly, was a joy!

Phena O'Boyle

Giving Up Smoking

Albert on his motorcycle

"Love is an outward and visible sign of an inward alloverness."

P eople give up smoking for a variety of reasons. I gave up smoking for love. It happened this way. At seventeen, I fell in love with a lovely girl about my own age. Now, this girl liked a man who smoked a pipe. She loved the smell of tobacco smoke – pipe smoke, that is. So, I started smoking a pipe. Well after about six months, romance faded. She went her way and I went mine – me, of course, still smoking my pipe, and even that changed after some months to cigarettes.

It is still amazing how events change history. Petrol which had been unavailable during the war came back on ration and I, being mad about motorbikes, borrowed money from my father and bought an ex army BSA. Miraculous is the word, going from the old push bike to these new-found wheels has to be one of the highlights of my life – I, with my pillion passenger, travel- ing as we did all over the country. It was wonderful, but there was a Catch 22 situation: money.

I talked to my father about reducing the amount I was paying him off the loan. What with tax, insurance and petrol expenses, I was having difficulty. He questioned me about the various ex- penses, especially about the petrol and then about the cost of ci- garettes. Well, the cost of petrol and cigarettes being about equal, it was easy to see that giving up cigarettes was the answer.

It could be said that I started smoking and gave up smoking for loves of a different kind.

Albert Connor

Kennedy's Cadets

Kennedy's Cadets

Ask anybody and they will remember where they were on that tragic day - 22nd Nov. 1963. For that was the day that President John F. Kennedy was shot in Dallas, Texas. But that day is particularly poignant for me. I had just left school that year and joined the Army as an Officer Cadet in the Military College, situated on the plains of the Curragh, Co. Kildare.

On that fateful Saturday night an urgent order went out for all Cadets to assemble in the drill hall. Calls were made to all the local cinemas and dance halls, ordering all Cadets to return to barracks. We thought World War III had broken out. The CO, Col Mattimoe, appeared in civvies, which was most unusual, and informed us that President Kennedy had been assassinated Furthermore, a request had been made by his widow, Jackie, for a contingent of Irish Cadets to be flown to Washington to act as an honour guard at his funeral. Kennedy had visited Ireland earlier that year and had been impressed by the complicated arms drill performed by the Cadets at Arbour Hill.

At this announcement there was a flurry of activity in the Cadet lines. Firstly, we had to draw out from the armory the old Lee Enfield 303 rifles specifically for this drill, called Queen Ann's Drill. Twenty six lucky Cadets were selected and flown off to Washington by Aer Lingus the next day. This was a huge honour for the cadet School, the Irish Army and the country as a whole. Historically this was the only time that a group of armed foreign soldiers were allowed on American soil. Many onlookers at the graveside were astonished at the strange uniforms, especially as the orders were given 'as Gaeilge.'

Mike Mahon

My Memories Of England

London

I n the late sixties, I left my home in Offaly and travelled by train to Dún Laoghaire and by ferry to Holyhead. It was a seven hour train trip to London Euston. With ten shillings and six pence in my pocket, I got the No. 30 bus to Hackney in east London to my aunt's home. It cost me six pence for the fare, which left me ten shillings to live on for the week.

I was in luck and I got a job the day after I arrived. After three days on the job, I asked the foreman would I get paid that week and to my horror I discovered I'd have to work a week in hand, but was told I could get a sub to keep me going. On that job they were all English except me and a man from Galway, who was about ten years older than me. This man told me that when he came to England there were signs outside building sites that no Irish and blacks need apply. Outside houses where they advertised rooms to let, it was the same story. He said to me that things were changing fast and in ten years time the Irish will be the top dogs. A lot of the men I worked with talked about the war that was still fresh in their minds, and felt they had got a raw deal and didn't get any help from the government on their return. They talked about the singer Vera Lynn and how she had kept their spirits up and would break into the song 'We'll Meet

Again.'

Four years later I worked in a job in Hatfield which was about 10 miles from London. I travelled on the train with a man from Jamaica who worked in the same job as me. We worked and travelled to the job for a year. He was a decent man and one evening after work as we travelled on the train he asked me to go for a pint later. We went into an Irish pub and as I was going up to get the drinks he said he'd get the first one because the Irish made the way for his nationality in England.

I returned to Ireland in the seventies and kept in touch with my Galway friend over the years. When I later went to London on visits, I visited him and one evening in the mid eighties, as we chatted, he reminded me of what he predicted. The Irish now had top jobs in England. He had two houses; one son worked in the City; another son was a manager for George Wimpy, and a daughter who was a solicitor.

Jim Browne

Fading Fighters

This fighter was reluctant. The tough kids had arrived in our back lane. They came from Clogher Road, newly built on the other side of the Grand Canal at Sally's Bridge. The attraction was our boxing ring which consisted of two ropes strung across between the walls of the lane making a square. McGuckian, their leader, declined a match with Turlough Breathnach, our star boxer. He pointed instead at me. Afraid to say that I was afraid, I held out my hands. Our coach and mentor, Benny Lynch did the taping and then laced on the gloves.

I went on a two fisted attack. It was easily dodged by McGuckian, who promptly planted a punch on my nose. A claret tap opened and I was honourably discharged. McGuckian was scarcely warmed up. He pointed at my pal, Eddie Walshe. Now Eddie was small and elusive. When things got tough, he went down, but he never stayed on the ground for the full count. His fight was lasting longer than mine, but eventually, he was trapped against the wall. Things looked desperate. Time for Plan B.

The wall formed the boundary of Eddie's house. Knowing exactly how hard to push, he bounced against the wicket gate and disappeared from sight into his own back garden. Gate slammed. Fight over. No escape for Billy McGuckian now. In a third fight, Turlough Breathnach took him apart with the consummate skill of a young Muhamed Ali.

Paddy Conneff

Looking At Terenure From The 1960s On

Terenure

L ooking at Terenure from the 1960's on, there are some changes compared with today but not huge. There is more traffic today and parking is difficult. It used to be possible to park outside 'H. Williams' easily and for free. It is now called 'Centra' and if parking is available, it has to be paid for. After shopping, it was quite easy to execute a U-turn and there was no central island in the way. Traffic coming from Rathgar could turn right at the crossroads. Now that is forbidden and traffic turning from other directions was not restricted from turning. Inside H. Williams there was a counter where bacon rashers could be sliced, and sausages were not pre-packaged.

There was a second grocery shop which was housed in the large building known as 'Flood's', which included the public house and a fish shop. The grocery shop still sold goods in a traditional fashion, which had largely died out. The shopper had to go to different counters and choose and pay for the goods at each counter. Sugar was weighed out and filled into special bags made of thick paper, often dark blue in colour. There were small bags which held one pound and larger bags which held two pounds of sugar. The top was folded deftly to seal in the sugar. Rashers and sausages were sold at another counter, and great cubes of butter were divided into pound and half pound rectangles, using two wooden butter clappers which cut and shaped the butter. Biscuits could be bought 'loose' from large, square tin boxes with glass windows and holding seven pounds of biscuits. Money for payment was handed over to the assistant who unscrewed a small container from an overhead cable into which he put the money together with the invoice and screwed it back on and pulled a pulley which shot it off to the cash office where it was recorded, change given and the whole lot sent back again to the assistant to hand to the customer. It took a long time to shop.

There was also a draper's shop called 'Bergin's' which had a long counter with four or more assistants behind it. This was a great shop to buy woollen yarn for knitting garments. The wool was kept in wooden cubby holes, which took up the entire wall behind the counter. Wrapping paper was on a roll with a bar to cut it and twine to tie was kept in a tin which had a hole in the lid through which it was pulled. 'Vaughan's' was the other big public house.

There was a serving attendant at the petrol pumps and these pumps stood on the footpath close to the curb. Now petrol cannot be bought in Terenure. Other services which have gone are the cobbler's, the 'Home Stores' which sold hardware needed for the home, the post office which was in 'O'Flanagans' news agency and 'Smith's' the pork butcher's where the full sides of pork could be seen hanging from hooks just inside the door and dripping onto the sawdust beneath.

The chip shop sold chips wrapped in newspaper and the shops used scales and brass weights and the currency was pounds, shillings and pence. The Gárda Station, though not gone, has vacated its little village type house on the Main Street, opposite the 'Terenure Inn' public house.

Last but not least, the 'Classic Cinema', fondly remembered as clean, well run and not too smoky has been replaced by 'Window Fashions' and, importantly the 'Terenure Enterprise Centre'.

Opal Peard

A Debt Repaid

Caughoo

On a lazy summer afternoon a friend of mine, John McCoy, and I were sitting outside our bowling club sipping pints and swopping yarns about events that had helped shape our lives. He came up with a story that topped any of mine.

In the 1940's John's grand uncle, Patrick Byrne, was employed as a night-watchman by Dublin Corporation. He had spent most of his life working as a labourer in the UK and Ireland. When he reached the age of 78, he settled for a job as a day-watchman on road works situated between Fairview and St. Lawrence Road. This consisted of a day and a half per week that paid him the princely sum of £1 4s.

During this time, Patrick lived alone in fairly frugal conditions in a small flat in Lower Ormond Quay. His niece, Bridie McCoy, John's mother, lived in Dundrum with her husband, a coalman, and their 14 children. Mrs McCoy's regular routine, after taking care of her children, was to take the bus into the city centre to visit her uncle, Patrick Byrne. There she washed, cleaned, cooked and cared for him.

Every year for 14 years, Patrick liked to buy two and a half tickets in the Irish Hospital Sweepstakes for the Aintree Grand

National. In 1947, using the nom-de-plume 'Black Cat', Patrick drew a horse – Caughoo who was trained on the sands in Sutton, Co. Dublin.

Caughoo was a rank outsider but Patrick refused all offers for a share in his ticket. On Saturday, March 29, 1947, Caughoo emerged from the gloom and mist of Aintree to romp home first past the post. The starting price was 100:1.

Suspicions were rife that the little horse hid behind a fence early on in the famous steeplechase, only emerging from his hiding place near the end of the race to romp home 20 lengths clear of the field.

The myth that Caughoo had cheated was entertained because thick fog obscured the Aintree course on the day and neither jumper or jockey, Eddie Dempsey, had ever raced in England before. However the myth was finally laid to rest when the Mirror newspaper published photographs of little Caughoo jumping Becher's Brook on two different occasions.

Caughoo had indeed proved a worthy winner.

Patrick's share of the winning prize was £25,000. Interviewed after the race, Patrick was matter-of-fact. 'I couldn't listen to the race 'cos I was working. So I sent a messenger to bring me the result, and then, when I knocked off work after 5 o'clock, I sent a wire to the Corporation to send a man in my place tomorrow.'

'Now,' he added: 'I think I have worked long enough.'

To put Patrick's winnings into perspective, it has been calculated, using the retail price index, that £25,000 in 1947 is worth over €800,000 in today's money.

Shortly after Patrick's win, there was a knock on the Mc-Coy's door in Dundrum. It was Patrick. He handed his niece a cheque for the full amount of his winnings! He hadn't forgotten his niece's kindness to him over the years. They bought a bigger bungalow in Beaumont Avenue and built an extension to house the 17 of them in more comfort. Patrick came to live with the McCoy's until he died there in his eighties.

John McCoy was able to attend the De La Salle secondary school in the area, and some of the children who hadn't been too well shod 'til then got new shoes for the first time.

'I have is a copy of the front page of the Sunday Independent of the following day, telling the story of Patrick's great win. Framed I have it. On the wall. In the same frame I have the original lodgement slip that was made out to Patrick's account for £25,000.'

John took a sip on his pint. His gaze took him across the green, beyond the bowlers in their whites, and into the past.

'Only for Patrick I wouldn't be here today.'

Rick Quinn

Retirement

Terenure Enterprise Centre

B etween 1958 and 2004, I worked as a statistician/economist at the Central Statistics Office and the Economic and Social Research Institute, both located in Dublin. During that time I also did contract work abroad on economic impacts of tourist expenditure in Malta, in Kenya, and also in Barbados where I spent the 1999-2000 period.

Starting with my full retirement about 2005, I had more time to get involved in other activities. Excellent courses on Information Technology (IT) were available at the Terenure Enterprise Centre, under the aegis of the 'Active IT Society' (AITS). I was able as an AITS member to complete the courses successfully and obtain the 'European Computer Driving Licence' (ECDL) certificate dated March 2009. This achievement gave me great satisfaction.

I could now start believing the proverb: 'All work and no play makes Jack a dull boy.' A wide range of leisure activities became possible. Having a small refracting telescope, I could try to see what the sky offered at night. I soon found myself writing a monthly column on this topic for the AITS blog spot, an ongoing and very enjoyable pastime. I use as background the monthly report of Ian Morison available on the internet. AITS Committee work and acting as a link with the AONTAS Community

Education Network, continue to take up some more of my time. These activities give me pleasure as further good uses of my leisure time. Creative writing is an added pleasure, by way of short stories and verse. These pieces appear in our AITS blog spot.

AITS have a sub-committee to arrange outings of interest. Some of our recent outings have been to Áras an Úachtaráin, to a Carlow museum, and to Belfast. I write a brief description of each of these events for our blog spot. Our July 2011 trip to Birr Castle proved very enjoyable to me, given my taste for astronomy. There we saw the famous telescope built and used by Lord Rosse in the 1840s. This telescope was at that time the world's largest.

Many older people give time to voluntary work for their various Churches. As a Catholic, I am involved with the World Apostolate of Fatima. This takes up some of my time, between what we do in Dublin and also nationally. It also means travel abroad to maybe one conference per year. I can truly summarise my situation by saying, 'Never a dull moment!'

Eamon Henry

A Day At The Races

I first learnt to ride a horse in Birmingham in the 60's. At my first lesson the instructor said to me in his military accent, 'I'll show you once and once only how to mount the horse.' I was petrified of him and the horse! However, once I got up and moved around the ring, I seemed to get the hang of it. At the end of the lesson, himself said to me, 'I can't believe you have never sat on a horse before.' I never knew whether he meant being Irish had something to do with it, or else I didn't do too bad for my first lesson. But the sheer joy of cantering around a riding ring initially and later out in the field and later still over the jumps was so exhilarating and unforgettable. But horse-racing became my real love of sport, though not as a participant – only as a punter.

Attendance at race meetings has been my life-long delight – going through the entrance gates on a good sunny day with a fair amount of Euro in my purse and, yes, I may win, lose or draw – that has always been my attitude. Called the Sport of Kings, incorporating the highest of society though I am always conscious I am just another punter and very often lucky.

It is fair to say that at any race meeting there is an invisible thread of horse-race interest running through the crowds. Everybody is there to see their favourite horse win; to check on the jockeys and to see what the bookies and tote odds are. You can turn to just anybody there, male or female and strike up a conversation without as much as a worry or embarrassment.

For me, there have been some great highlights at horserace meetings over the years. I suppose Royal Ascot and Cheltenham in England and the Curragh, Leopardstown and the Galway Festival would be the most outstanding. The thrill of seeing the Royal Family drive down the course at Royal Ascot Ladies' Day and later on in the day, to pick up Lester Pigott's three winners and hear 'the 'poor old bookie' say when I went to collect, 'Blimey, not you again' always sticks in my mind. And as for Cheltenham's Festival on Gold Cup day, to witness your winning horse storm up that famous hill to the winning post – the roar of the crowd, the thunder of the horses' hooves, hands, brochures, hats in the air and your own heart in your mouth with excitement - yes, yes, your horse has won the Gold Cup simply awesome!!

But the Irish race meetings have really been my favourites with Galway's July Festival taking the honours. Having attended there almost all my adult life, taking the Jackpot home with me on a few occasions with the brothers and nephews looking on in amazement. You could say, I suppose, like they thought, 'what did I know about racing?' Well, apart from the Jackpot, I'm familiar with betting ways of the Exacta, Tricast, Each Way and my personal favourite – the Lucky 15 – you pick four horses in four different races. With these, I've had some very exciting occasions when it came to paying out my winnings. One was in Cheltenham, when the teller said to me, in her clipped accent. 'Oh, dearie, I haven't enough cash, I'll have to go and get more.' I turned to the man behind me, dressed like an advert for Sandyman's Port and said, 'Gosh, it looks as if I've broken the Bank of England!'

Another occasion, in the West of Ireland – the teller said,

'You'll have to wait 10 minutes before I can unlock the safe, I haven't enough cash to pay you out.' Music to my ears!

So my sporting life was and still is 'A Day at the Races'.........

Maureen Maloney

Free At Last

Margaret – 'Free at Last'

F ree at last! This mantra was racing through my mind as I hopped out of bed for my last day at work. The opportunity of early retirement had presented itself and without too much deep thought or perusal, I embraced the chance of a whole new future. I still had my health and sanity and had nothing to lose, or had I?

As I drove to school that sunny June morning, I pondered the decades I had spent in the classroom - the lives I had touched, and most of all I hoped I had made a difference. I considered the choices that lay ahead--opportunities to travel at off peak times, catch up with old friends, visit family etc. My friends, colleagues and pupils gave me a great send off and I left with a lovely warm feeling in my heart.

The euphoria lasted a few years!! I travelled to many far flung places. Most enjoyable was a trip to South Africa, made all the sweeter by the fact that we went in September, when I should have been back in school.

Only one snag attends this new phase in my life: there is no denying, I am getting older!! People no longer remark "you are too young to be retired." I had to leave my comfort zone and bring some discipline back into my life. I got involved in various types of parish work and am a member of ASITS here in Terenure, which has opened up several new opportunities to me. I am very grateful for this and I am now computer literate!!

I look forward to the future and thank God for these happy and hopefully healthy years. I feel greatly blessed.

Margaret Magee

Ireland's Only Hope

FCA Tank

T his is what we were called by the local wags who should
have known better. It was the time of the Cuban Missile
Crisis, and I decided in a fit of patriotism to join the FCA (which
was the Army reserves) and defend the country to the last drop
of my blood.

To this end we were issued with uniforms consisting of a
snot green tunic, matching baggy trousers, reddish brown boots
and gaiters and to complete the ensemble, beret style headgear.
Now while most armies had camouflage uniforms, the Irish
Army was different; our tunics were festooned with rows of
brightly shining brass buttons, presumably to ensure that the enemy
could see us clearly.

We paraded every Sunday mornings and Tuesday nights for
training. Initially this was marching around the parade and per-
forming various drills, which is usually called 'square bashing.'
After some months we were issued with rifles. These were .303
Lee Enfields, and we practised loading, aiming and firing with
dummy rounds. Finally, the great day arrived. We were to be al-
lowed to fire live bullets on the target range. We were brought up
to Ticknock, in the Dublin Mountains, and took up firing posi-
tions. Just as the officer in charge, Lieut. Duffy, gave the order to

fire, a lone sheep hove into view. 'Fire!' he yelled, and we all let fly. The unlucky sheep disintegrated in a hail of bullets. Duffy let loose a string of army invectives and threw his hands in the air. 'Cease firing. Cease firing........stop. I say stop!' We were all put on a charge of destroying Government property and fined 2/3d old money.

Annual training camp was in Kilkenny barracks, and there were units from all over the country. We were issued with steel helmets, webbing equipment and haversacks. One exercise we had was what the Army called 'field craft.' This entailed crawling around the countryside, trying to remain as inconspicuous as possible. To this end, we were instructed to cover ourselves in leaves, branches and other shrubbery. The idea was to blend in as far as possibly with the local foliage. But one genius, of doubtful sexuality, decorated himself in brightly coloured wild flowers.. When the platoon sergeant saw this multi-coloured apparition, he went apoplectic and roared at the poor unfortunate individual, 'Private, where do you think you're going? To an effing wedding?' 'Right, full pack drill and rifles. See that hill with the gorse bushes? I want the lot of you up there,' Captain Ryan roared, 'and back before tea time.'
'Sir, do you mean that big mountain on the horizon?'
'Don't try to be smart with me, Private Malone. Now move it.'

We headed off at a brisk pace, all one hundred and twenty of us. But soon many of us started to lag behind and we got the idea to drop into a ditch or hollow in the ground out of sight and join the rest on the way back. Unfortunately, for us Ryan had positioned an NCO at the summit under orders to take the names of those who made it to the top. The rest of us who had skived off were stuck with guard duty and fatigues for the remainder of the camp.

To this day, any time I see that TV programme 'Dad's Army',
I am reminded of my time in An Fórsa Cosanta Áitiúl.

Mike Mahon

As I Get Older

Albert in the AITS computer room

A s I get older - and having retired - I find that I am not expected to be able to do things that I would have done heretofore, but in fact I now find that I have much more time to devote to things that I enjoy doing, like playing golf, lawn bowling, swimming, travel, oil painting, playing and listening to music etc. I am now able to offer my services to projects like the Active IT Society. I am also involved in running the local U3A retirement group and am a member of a PROBUS club.

Some amusing things can happen as a result of peoples' perception of age. Let me explain. My wife, unfortunately, suffered from Alzheimer's, a progressive sickness, which required an increased amount of care as time went by; a job that eventually took all my time, like twenty four hours a day, seven days a week. I had no time to play golf or join any clubs. After about seven years, I became ill as a result of stress and my doctor advised me that I should look for a good nursing home, which I did.

Eventually, my wife was transferred to this home and I was able to recover my health. A short time later, I paid a visit to my doctor for a check-up. He gave me a thorough going over and pronounced me fit. He then advised me to join clubs and take part in other activities.

By the way, he said; 'This is the time to look up all your old friends.' 'Doctor,' I said, 'You are a man of forty. I am seventy nine; all my old friends are dead.'

PS: Actually, it's not the years in your life that count; it's the life in your years.

Albert Connor

Meeting Samuel Beckett

Beckett by Brian Breathnach

Each time I visit Paris I try to return to the small café at the Hotel PLM on the Boulevard Saint Jacques in the fourteenth Arrondissement where I met Samuel Beckett in March 1987. I had written to Beckett requesting a meeting after making some paintings inspired by his work. He mesmerised me, and his life and work have become a great source of inspiration for my work as a visual artist and have helped me a great deal on a personal level by means of a catharsis. That time we sat facing each other at a small round marble toped table. Beckett was frail and friendly - he would be 82 years old the following month - and when the double espresso coffee arrived he was unable to open the paper sachet of sugar cubes. He looked down upon the sachet of sugar cubes with a sadness as it lay on the table, defeated by such a small task, 'His past hands, after all they had done.' I offered my assistance to open the sugar, which was accepted, and this provided a human touch which opened our conversation.

We spent an hour together in that small café and we spoke about James Joyce and Dublin and the difficult times being experienced in Ireland during the 1980's. 'I believe all the young people are getting out,' he remarked. We spoke about painting and about Jack B. Yeats and he told me he used to have two paintings by Yeats but had given both of them away. I asked him why he gave his paintings away and he replied: 'It's not easy getting rid of things. One accumulates a great deal in a lifetime.' He asked about my work and commented on one of my painting which I had sent him a photograph of. He made an observation about the painting which paid me an enormous compliment and displayed the encyclopaedic knowledge and understanding of art history he possessed by identifying the specific influence on my work.

I was amazed by the gentle courtesy and kind curiosity of this artistic colossus in whose company I found myself and I was struck by the modesty and humility he exuded. He seemed to be in the flesh even more like himself than the photographs could ever have prepared me for. His face was pale as though sculpted in white marble, each of those familiar lines deeply incised as though carved by Michelangelo. His eyes were a bright sky blue and as deep as the ocean. They fixed me in their gaze and seemed to see deep into my mind before drifting off out through the window into the Parisian streets and up over the roof tops and onwards into infinity and then back again. We chatted casually and I attempted to avoid asking him any probing or foolish questions about his work but everything he said sounded like his work, in the way that he looked like his work, and in the end he had become his work. I asked him was he still writing to which he replied, 'No. I am kept busy with the menial tasks of life that keep us going.' And then he looked at me with an expression of hopelessness and said forlornly as he shook his head, 'Dreadful problem with the mail.' Eventually our conversation turned to sport which Beckett was greatly interested in. He reminded me that Ireland would be playing rugby against France at Lansdowne Road the following Saturday. 'If France win they will achieve the Grand Slam,' he noted. I wondered if perhaps such a game would split his loyalties and I enquired coyly: 'And who will you be cheering for?' He replied dead pan and looking straight at me. 'I won't be cheering.' This raised a warm smile from me and goes a long way to explain why I have been cheering for Samuel Beckett ever since; the man and artist who teaches us to smile at our misfortunes and to laugh at our miseries.

Brian Breathnach

How I Met Eileen

Kevin and Eileen

My first experience of love was in my home where I was raised with wonderful care and kindness. This developed in me a great respect for women, especially motherhood, that has remained with me all my life.

As a teenager I was cursed with shyness that left me very awkward in the company of girls. My first date didn't happen until I was twenty. Over the next few years, girls didn't play a big part in my life, as I was much too involved in sport, playing Gaelic Football and handball and stewarding in Croke Park.

My football club, Clanna Gael, held dances every Wednesday night in Parnell Square and gave us complimentary tickets to distribute. I gave them mostly to girls. I always gave some to Eileen, whom I met when delivering bread and cakes to her aunt's shop where she worked. With Eileen and me it wasn't love at first sight. It was something that grew over time. Her honesty made a big impression on me. If I ever forgot to charge for something she'd tell me and pay me next time. It also helped she had a lovely figure and was very good looking. In September 1961 we were married, forty-nine years later we are still holding hands ... most of the time! We have five adult children, all married, and twelve grandchildren. Little Ella, our great grandchild, sadly she did not survive.

As for my good wife Eileen, she is my rock, companion and everything that is good and wholesome in my life. It also helps that she is a wonderful cook and housekeeper. Our love boat weathered a few bad storms but now has reached calm and peaceful waters with sunshine most days.

Why have I been so lucky in love and life?

Kevin McGrath

My New Baby Brother

I have many memories of my childhood, but there is one that stands out vividly. I was only three years of age. My sister and I were sent into our neighbour, Mrs. Balfe, for tea. I liked her very much and she taught me how to knit. I was not happy, however, when we had to sleep there, as I missed my own bed, but my sister, Marie was kind to me.

At this point, I fear my memory has failed me, but I then remember being brought up to a big house by my Dad. We were brought up the stairs and into a beautiful bedroom, where to my surprise, I saw my Mother in bed and beside her was a little white cot. As I looked into the cot, my Mother said: 'Give your baby brother a kiss'. I was very excited and then a lovely nurse with red curly hair and white dress brought me out and gave me red lemonade and a lollipop.

After that my memory failed me again and I just remember being at home again with my sister and big brother and my Mother sitting beside the fire, nursing my lovely baby brother.

Eileen Williamson

Monte Carlo Or Bust

We were staying in Cannes for a week. My school principal, teachers and admin staff, myself among them, were having a ball, sunning ourselves on the beach in luxury. Waiters brought our lunch while we gazed out at the tranquil blue sea dotted with yachts of various sizes gleaming in the sun. Tomorrow, we said, we would take a trip to Monaco and Monte Carlo. Looking around the luxurious castle guarded so colourfully, we were enchanted with its style and felt the presence of Princess Grace in every glorious room.

On then to Monte Carlo – just up my street I thought – as we made for the Casino! Once inside, the adrenalin started to flow. All eyes on me. Would I show them how the 'slot machines' worked. 'OK,' I said, 'Here goes.' You put your coin into the machine, press the button and there's your winnings. It will come in the shape of a paper docket with your grand total,' I said. 'You than take it to the teller who will pay out!' So, now all hands on deck. All seated at the various machines. 'Right, put your coin in, like I showed you. Press the button and wait for your winnings!' 'Now, all done.' Cries and shouts of disappointment from all sides. Not one of our group received a winning docket – except myself. Disbelief all round. How could that be? 'Well, that is what is known as luck,' I said. My docket showed a very good profitable figure. I had to show it to each of my friends, before they would believe me. Then up to the teller, wait while he checked the docket and then with a crooked smile he paid me out my winnings! I stood counting out my notes while my friends crowded around me. Such laughter and cries of disbelief. And they chorused: 'The drinks are on you tonight.'

Maureen Maloney

An Embarrassing Moment

Church of the Annunciation. Rathfarnham

I n the early sixties we moved from Ranelagh to Rathfarnham. Our beautiful old house was proving difficult to live in with a young family. It was piercingly cold in winter and in all seasons the endless flights of stairs to the bathroom at the top with babies in tow had become too difficult to sustain.

A new problem that presented with the move was the fact that only rarely did a bus cross Templeogue Bridge and from being within walking distance of the City in Ranelagh, I was now truly out in the sticks. There was only one solution. I had to learn to drive.

For the marriage to survive, dearly beloved wasn't an option as tutor, but a good friend Noel stepped up to the mark. We had three or four lessons up around Firhouse and later on to Bohernabreena. Noel wasn't familiar with the narrow hairpin at the waterworks, and to be truthful neither was I, but to our mutual astonishment I negotiated it with reasonable ease. Mass goers, and the queues of people waiting to board for the return journey up the mountains could not be imagined in this day and age. Added to this was the fact that cars had been parked literally bumper to bumper with my little mini. I was well. This I think was due in no small measure to my vast experience on the dodgems in Bray.

Full of confidence I decided to take the car to Mass in Rathfarnham the following Sunday. The old hump-back bridge was still in situ and in order to avoid it, I drove up Ballyroan Road and down Willbrook Road and could then return home by way of left hand turns to Butterfield Avenue.

I arrived early for 10am Mass and parked with vast spaces to front and rear. What I hadn't thought about was 11am Mass. As I came out of the church, the Rockbrook buses were offloading dozens of Mass goers and the queues of people waiting to board for the return journey up the mountains could not be imagined in this day and age. Added to this was the fact that cars had been parked literally bumper to bumper with my little mini. I was well and truly trapped!!

Some problems in life need drastic solutions. I approached the bus inspector who was directing traffic and asked for help. He had a quick look and acknowledged my dilemma, but admitted that he actually didn't drive. Seeing my desperation, he promised to help.

By this time the buses had filled and were starting to pull away. With a wave he flagged one down, had a quick word with the driver who left his seat and came across to my car. Curious passengers stood up and crowded the windows and the remaining people on their way into Church waited and watched as the bus driver sat into my car and expertly eased it out. In full view of the assembled audience he handed back the keys to me with a broad grin and a kindly pat on the shoulder.

Fia Weber

Congo

I had been working as a trainee salesman for an office suppliers' company in the East End of London. I was not very excited with the prospect of spending the rest of my life selling paper, ink and copy machines. I had a CPL (Civil Pilot's Licence) and this seemed infinitely more exciting. So, when I saw an ad looking for pilots in the Congo, I immediately applied. I was delighted to get an airline ticket via Brussels to Kinshasa for a job interview, and resigned there and then. I flew from London to Brussels and presented myself at the Air Congo office. I was greeted by the local manager, a caricature of Idi Amin, who I remember had two beautiful long legged secretaries straight out of Bay Watch. I was given a wad of Congolese Francs and headed of for Kinshasa.

The Congo had been a Belgian colony and recently obtained independence, resulting in a fierce tribal war as the province of Katanga tried to accede. There were six other potential applicants on that flight and on arrival we were met by the Chief pilot, a dour South African. He informed us we would be required to do an interview, a flight test and a medical, but, unfortunately, he could not offer us a job immediately. Air Congo had a huge fleet of piston-engine DC4's, 6's and 7's, but most of them were grounded for lack of spares. En masse we refused to do a medical when we saw conditions at the hospital. It was filthy and we all had valid European medical certificates. So, we were interviewed and all passed the flight test OK. But, as there was only one flight a week back to Brussels, we had a few days to hang around. One day, a few of us were sitting out on the balcony of the airport terminal, sipping beers and discussing where to go next. One of the guys stood up, produced a camera and proceeded to photograph a landing aircraft. Now, this is one thing you do not do at an African airport. We warned him but he

brushed aside our advice. Sure enough, he was suddenly sur-
rounded by a gang of soldiers brandishing sub-machine guns and
hustled off roughly. The rest of us sat quietly until they had
gone; then rushed down to the Chief Pilot's office. He let out a
string of invectives, donned his uniform cap, and rushed off
downtown in his jeep to rescue the poor unfortunate.

While at the terminal, I had noticed that there were other air-
craft at the far side of the airport. Thinking it might be a cargo
operation with possible jobs, I decided to investigate. I obviously
could not cross the airport, so the only way was to walk around
the perimeter, which was a good few miles in the tropical heat.
On getting there, there were a few decrepit hangars and a selec-
tion of all sorts of aircraft and helicopters. There was a bunch
of guys in a motley selection of military style uniforms sitting in
deck chairs sunning themselves, slugging beer and smoking what
I took to be pot. It was a scene straight out of MASH. When I
enquired if there were any pilot jobs, I was greeted by hoots of
laughter. 'No,' one of them replied. 'Not unless you want your
butt shot off. See - this is a military operation, top secret. We're
all mercenary pilots. We support whoever pays us.' They were
all American, and I guess running some sort of covert operation
for the Special Forces or the CIA. I left Kinshasa a few days
later and arrived back in Brussels, broke and disheartened. I still
had a large amount of Congolese francs and when I tried to
change them at the bank was told they were worthless.

Mike Mahon

The Most Unforgettable Person I've Met

Dr George Otto Simms

I had changed to a new school when I was nearly eight years old. It was the school connected to the Church of Ireland Teachers' Training College and was in Kildare place off Kildare Street.

One day we were told that we would be going to the Chapel for a service. This was a small chapel for the student teachers. The light-coloured oak pews or stalls lined the short aisle facing each other. Then Mr. Simms came in and we all stood up. He was very young, I thought, (thirty-six) and had dark hair and a long face. Long faces, I had decided, were a sign of holiness. He possessed a special smile unique to him which seemed to brighten his face. He was of slim build and gentle manner with a delightful speaking voice. When I was eight it mattered to me how people spoke. It mattered that they didn't rasp or grate or run their words together. He was of course the Reverend Mr. Simms, Chaplain – secretary to the Training College and also, I am told, Principal in practice though not in name. I remember that he preached a sermon which was a story I couldn't wait to tell my

mother about. I have no memory of the content of this or sub-
sequent sermons, but I have learned since that he was the author
of children's stories, including 'Exploring the Book of Kells.'
He was an academic and a man of great intellect. He studied at
Trinity College and held a doctorate in Divinity. He was a fluent
Irish speaker among other attributes but he was never over-
whelming. Instead, as a great teacher he brought people with
him.

My next memory of the late George Otto Simms was in 1956
when he was the newly appointed Church of Ireland Archbishop
of Dublin. He attended as Guest Speaker a prize-giving at Alex-
andra College in Earlsfort Terrace, which is now the site of the
Conrad Hotel. I was a Leaving Certificate student there at the
time. He spoke with charm and grace and brevity. Brevity is im-
portant to students at prize-giving, as the "also-rans" will testify.
After the ceremony I was intrigued to see the Archbishop on the
pavement outside the building wearing formal Ecclesiastical
dress. He was a neat slim figure, dressed in gaiters and apron.
He wore a clerical shirt with the pectoral cross and dog collar
along with breeches over which was the knee length apron which
would have been tied at the back and a broad cummerbund at his
waist. His legs were encased in tight fitting gaiters which were
buttoned from knee to ankle and he wore neat pointed toed shoes
with buckles. A frock coat with buttons and a mandarin collar
was the final garment. This form of dress devised for horse rid-
ing has died out.

As the years went by he became Archbishop of Armagh and
Primate of All Ireland. However my last memory is when he
had retired he gave a talk in the Parochial Hall to the Parishion-
ers of Zion Church in Bushy Park Road and their friends. He
held us enthralled by his description of the Book of Kells, which

is in Trinity College Library. His enthusiasm fired our imagina-
tions as he opened our eyes to its richness of colour and to the
intricacies of the patterns used to decorate the capital letters of
the text and to the pictures of human faces, animals and plant
life that was there. He spoke of finding fish and snakes and
goats and wolves and more woven into the text and decorations.
Some of these had symbolic meaning as, for example, a diagram
of a fish was used to represent Jesus Christ. He spoke of the
amusing things which were drawn by monks, who he thought
must have had a sense of humour. There is, for example, a de-
piction of a cat with two mice sitting on its back. Wouldn't chil-
dren enjoy that? Walt Disney you weren't the first!

George Otto Simms. 4th July1910 - 15th November 1991.

Opal Peard

The Synge Street Debating Society 1953/1954

The old Synge Street School

In the autumn of 1953, Brother Bill O'Leary made an appearance in the room where the debates were held. After the Auditor, Chris Batt, called for and failed to get nominations for the post of corresponding secretary, I received a push in the back from Bill, who then led the clapping, and our hero was elected to the secretary's position unopposed.

When revealed, the work required was frightening. A seventeen year old boy, with no money in his pocket and no telephone in the home, had the task of contacting eminent past pupils seeking to get a guest chairman for a debate in the school once a fortnight. By way of assistance, some street wise classmates took me out to teach me how to use a public telephone without money. It was called the back-dialling system, and I confess that I tried it once. When I was halfway through the process, the operator cut in to say that she knew what I was at and that a squad car was on the way. I took off at a sprint and did not rest until I was safe at my own fireside. Now I would be forced to raid my meagre personal piggy bank to finance the job.

I learned the list of famous past pupils. It included

Cornelius Ryan, war correspondent and author of 'The Longest Day.' In addition, David Kelly, Donal Donnelly, Milo O'Shea and Jack McGowran of acting fame, Mr. Chaim Hertzog, later to be President of Israel, Liam Cosgrave TD, later to be Taoiseach, Joseph Plunkett, author of 'Strumpet City' and many others, some of whom I would come to meet later.

There were several 'Thanks but no thanks' from targeted past pupils. This was at first devastating and then merely discouraging. But overall the exercise was positive. Despite many setbacks, Éamon Andrews of BBC fame, Cearbhall Ó Dálaigh, later to be President of Ireland and Richie Ryan, eventually an Auditor of the European Court - among several others - were all very kind to me and agreed to come and be celebrity chairman at our debate.

On the nights of the great debates, I did not get to speak on the school team. But I did have the duty of welcoming the guest dignitary. And on conclusion of the evening, I would propose a vote of thanks to the visiting chairman for generously giving of his time. It was to prove a positive influence in later life:

'Stand up and say only what needs to be said.'

Paddy Conneff

On The Way Home From School

Aidan O'Hara

W e saw many strange and wonderful sights in the skies over Muff during the last two years of World War 2 when we were going to school. Lough Foyle stretched out before us and on its broad bosom sailed war ships and submarines of the British, American and Canadian navies, and overhead squadrons of Spitfires and bombers of the RAF practised their dogfights and bombing runs to the amazement and delight of us youngsters. On our way home one afternoon we saw a seaplane landing on Lough Foyle, stop for a while and then take off again. This was something entirely new and a tale for us to tell our parents when we got home. When we turned right at Harkin's forge and were just about at Candless's Lane (there were many forms of that lane's name), Master Kirwan whizzed past us on his bike and headed down the lane, shouting out something about a plane crash in Kilderry Wood. Our mother insisted we have our dinner first before letting us loose, and soon we were hightailing it for the 'the Plantin', as we called Kilderry Wood.

I shall never forget standing right alongside the wrecked and burning Spitfire sticking out of the ploughed-up earth at the edge of a clearing where it had nose-dived into the ground. The scene and the smells of the crash site are still with me today. It seems that, for whatever reason, the pilot had to bail out and the plane flew around for some time over Muff and 'the Plantin' before coming in low over fields near the wood, zooming up once more and eventually plummeting to earth. My final memory of that event were the mixed feelings I had when I learned that my father, a member of An Garda Síochána, was to stay on duty at the crash site during the night.

To my way of thinking it gave him – and by extension, myself – a degree of some importance, but at the same time I was concerned that he might be in some danger at that scene of devastation and destruction.

Aidan O'Hara

A Childhood Memory

Maureen's family

I don't eat either mushrooms or blackberries. Why? Because when I was a child I got too much of them. My brothers used to go rabbit hunting quite a lot and would bring home to my mother 'loads' of mushrooms and blackberries they had picked from around the fields of the farm where we lived in Kildare. My mother would then make a meal out of the mushrooms by frying them in butter in the pan, and make a blackberry pie with apples from our own orchard. I got too much of each and to this day I will not eat either.

My father had a wonderful orchard and vegetable garden where he spent all his spare time. It was the envy of the neighbours! He had raspberries, strawberries, red and blackcurrants and vegetable marrows as well as the usual vegetable garden fare. There were several very good eating apples trees and each of my brothers had their own. And I had mine, which had Golden Delicious apples that only ripened in the autumn when all the others had been picked and eaten. Every year I used to be so proud of my tree and its golden apples. My brother would be forever coaxing me to let them have some as all theirs were gone.

Sadly, the orchard is no longer there. I remember going back years later to view the house and garden and almost crying on seeing the garden all levelled. But I can still see, in my mind's eye, my father working away with his back bent in that garden and can almost smell the apple pie cooking on the coal range we had in those days.

Not so long ago, Fr. Joe Ryan from Terenure, now sadly deceased, with whom my brothers went to school in Kildare, said to me: 'Maureen, I have a confession to make to you.'
'Oh, surely not, Father,' I said. 'Should it not be the other way around?' 'No. No,' he said. "I must confess that I stole apples out of your father's garden.' He shook his broad shoulders with laughter – no doubt with the childhood memory of it all!!

Maureen Maloney

Penny

Opal Peard

A span of fifteen years is a long time. I made a phone call. 'Will Jane be in on Tuesday as usual?' I asked.
'Yes indeed and Monday and Wednesday next week too.'
'I want to make an appointment. Please tell Jane I will bring Penny in to see her but this time I will not bring Penny home again.'

A little black 'Jack Russell' type mongrel with no appearance to recommend her had touched many hearts. Fifteen years ago my son phoned, 'Mum, last night as I closed my hall door a lovely little puppy followed me in. She seemed very hungry and I gave her my rashers to eat as I had nothing else to give her. Could you possibly come over and take her to your house overnight because, as you know, I have some perspective buyers coming to look over my house and a stray puppy in a cardboard box doesn't look too good?'

Over I went and found this appalling looking little animal, skeletal in appearance which fitted on the palm of my hand and whose very long legs dangled down. I knew the first thing I had to do was to take this pup to the vet. I rang to tell him he would be shocked, but not to blame me for what he would see. 'This is either a very sick dog or she is on the point of starvation,' the vet observed. 'As a matter of fact she is on the point of starvation. She has been brought up by the boot and that is why she is so gentle.' We had a discussion about what to do and, in the end, he gave me some suitable food, and I took this caricature of a dog home to mind for the time being. I had to bring her regularly to the Veterinary Practice. My own vet, who had been on holidays at the time, took one look at her and his face contorted in anger. 'Where did you get this dog from,' he demanded. He relaxed when I explained. From then on she improved, and I realised I couldn't let her go to someone else. She was quite wild and wouldn't make eye contact. She would only drink rainwater from puddles, and she would make a little dust bed in clay under the hedge to lie in. She did not like men in heavy black shoes, but she would leap across the room to sit on my father's knee.

As time went by, the children from the Presentation Convent School nearby learned to enjoy stroking her soft coat. Apparently, she was every child's mental picture of what a little dog should look like. It was interesting to see her sitting with the circle of grandchildren watching television. They often talked to her as one of them and never seemed to notice that she was not vocal. One child might have an arm around her, and another might have the dog sitting on her knee. She was great at catching balls and would bring them back to drop at our feet.

As the years went by she grew more sedate. She began to sleep more and to become grey round the muzzle. She wandered off and got lost a couple of times and we had to send out search parties. Recently the signs of ageing became very evident. She was slow and careful on the stairs. She needed more company. She required more veterinary care. 'Why don't you put her down?' I was asked. 'Because she is happy and not in pain and because she trusts me, and I will not betray her trust.

She is checked by the vet every three months and I hope she will slip away naturally, but if not, when the time comes we will do the right thing.'

We warned the grandchildren and adults that really Penny was very old now. She had become like a baby. I carried her to her bed and she would snuggle down with a sigh and what looked like a little smile. In the morning she would struggle to leave her bed. I knew she wanted a long sleep. I have a lovely sympathy card from the vet. 'It had all been very peaceful,' she wrote. 'Humane Euthanasia' is the official term. 'Were you very sad, Grand mum?' my Granddaughter enquired. 'A little sad but happy that Penny is where she wants to be.' With that my Granddaughter skipped off.

Opal Peard

My Working Life

One of Maureen's pupils

My grandfather was principal of a local school, so it is no surprise that several of his grandchildren are in the teaching profession. His great grandson recently secured a teaching post in exactly the same school - 65 years on!

I never seriously considered any career other than teaching and was elated when I was accepted *into* Sion Hill to train as a Home Economics teacher. I did a year's substitution in Muckross Park. The first morning was nerve wracking. You knew instantly the pupils were going to put you through your paces before accepting you. Soon, I got used to being on the other side of the desk. I shared a flat nearby with another newly qualified teacher, and we shared and compared classroom experiences each evening.

The following year, I moved to a lovely small school in Crumlin, where I remained for 23 years. I loved everything about my job. The nuns in charge were caring and kind. The staff was friendly and young. The pupils were full of life and I enjoyed their wit, humour and colourful expressions. My work conditions were excellent and I have many happy memories of days trips, school tours, sports days and the fun we had. Sadly an announcement was made that the school was closing down.

We were redeployed and so began a new chapter in my working life. I spent the following 14 years in Clondalkin. The contrast was great. Huge numbers of students and staff. Suddenly, life became turbo-charged. There was never enough time to get all the work done!,

Looking back on it now, I can say my working life had its challenging and difficult moments but it was never dull!

Margaret Magee

Air Tours

Ulster Pride – Mike's plane in the London to Sydney Air Race

We were all excited when the managing director told us that we were getting a new fleet of aircraft, but less so when they arrived. They were the Bristol Britannias, the first four-engined turbo-prop aircraft built by the Brits. They were in service with the RAF Transport Command and finally retired after many years. Of course, Paddy's airline bought them at knock down prices. Their electrical system was a nightmare, components were prone to failures and spares were in short supply, as they were no longer in production. The control surfaces were 'free floating', and in icing conditions froze up solid and became immoveable. The only way out of this was to descend the aircraft to a warmer altitude and hope to reach this before coming in contact with the land or sea. At that time, aviation in Ireland was regulated by the Department of Transport and Power, and the aircraft and crews were constantly monitored by their inspectors. They were all civil servants, and the crews maintained that the wheel barrow had been invented to teach these guys to walk on their hind legs

Milan Airport lay on the southern side of the Alps, and on a departure from that airport heading north, aircraft were required to reach a certain altitude to clear the mountains. Now this was no problem to modern jet aircraft, but to our clapped out Britannias it was impossible to climb directly on course, so we would have to orbit until we got sufficient altitude to proceed. This caused Swiss Air Traffic Control many problems. Their methodical controllers just could not understand our plight and dreaded hearing our call sign. We called ourselves 'Paddy Powerless Airlines.'

On these flights climbing out of Milan, it was one of the copilot's responsibilities to ensure that the aircraft was being pressurised correctly, by gradually closing an outflow valve at his feet. One new co-pilot forgot to do this and the aircraft continued to climb unpressurised. The Captain, in the left seat, failed to notice and continued to smoke heavily on his Blue Gitannes. He was a big heavy man with a bread and jam face , and it was only when the Flight Engineer noticed the back of his head was turning blue and that he was coughing continuously that disaster was averted. The Captain was actually expiring due to lack of oxygen.

Mike Mahon

My Singing Career Today

John MacNally, his wife Anne, daughter Elizabeth and son, Justin

M y singing career still goes on with great gusto. As I live in Australia, most of my concerts throughout the year happen here. Most recently, I completed a 14 concert tour of the theatres in Queensland within a period of 18 days. This tour started by plane from Sydney and continued with a 4,500 km drive between the venues.

To give a typical example: my musical director Anne and myself arrive at the theatre two hours before show time to organise lights, sound and stage settings. As the theatre staff are all professionals, this does not take too long. Then we set about getting a balance between the voice and the music. This also serves to loosen up my voice with a good rehearsal. When we finish all that, we retire to the dressing room to discuss and fix the running order as the show lasts for about one and a half hours. During this time the audience arrives and is treated to a cup of tea or coffee and a biscuit. We then do the show and afterwards I go out front to the foyer to meet the people, chat to them and sign autographs. Anne has a table set up with all the CD's and DVD's for those who may be interested. After all that is finished, we pack up and proceed to the next theatre. This week - July 27th,

28th and 29th 2011 – for instance, I go to Canberra to sing three concerts at the Q Theatre. CD's are very popular and I just recently recorded a new one titled 'Melodies of Love', which contains my present favourite song 'You Raise Me Up'. I have a series of concerts coming up in America and I always look forward to that. On occasions I sing concerts in Dublin.

In total I have released 40 CD's and also a three-film DVD and I make a selection of these available after each concert.

John MacNally

My Sporting Life

Jim's Sporting Life

I first got interested in sport when I was eight years old. A group of us started playing cricket in a field near my home. We made bats from spare wood we found. There was one lad a few years older than the rest of us that taught us a bit about the game. He had learned it from his grandfather who had worked in England in his youth. One person would serve the ball to one of the batsmen and the trick was to hit the ball as far as you could to get as many runs as you could before the ball came back. We enjoyed playing this game for hours on evenings and weekends.

When we got a little older we played Gaelic football on the same field. Then later on I got interested in both football and hurling, first in local games and then following my native Offaly team. They did not have much success at first, but then in 1971 they had the breakthrough. The footballers won two in a row. They beat Galway in 1971 and Kerry in a replay in 1972. When we won the first all Ireland there was great excitement in Tullamore, the bonfires burned all day on the Monday and all through the night.

When the Offaly hurlers won in 1981 for the first time the celebrations were in Birr, the home town of hurling in Offaly. That game was won in the last minute; there was a scramble in the square and Johnny Flaherty palmed the ball to the net. There was great excitement for another two days of celebrations.

The footballers won again in 1982 in a very exiting game against a great Kerry team that was going for five in a row, Offaly were two points down with one minute to go. Liam O'Connor got a free out on the forty and sent a high ball in that was caught by Seamus Darby. He kicked the ball to the roof of the net. Kerry was stunned, and to this day Mick O'Dwyer says he will never forget that day. I went to football and hurling matches in Croke Park over the years. I met up with a lot of people from home and people I worked with. We would go for a few pints and have the crack, talking about the matches.

In the last few years, I took up golf which is very enjoyable. Every time I go out on the golf course I get about three hours of fresh air and great fun. I play in Stepaside Golf course a lot, in Lucan Golf course and the Southside Golf course.

Jim Browne

A Game I Played When I Was Young

A t the Presentation Secondary school in Baltinglass, camogie was perhaps the main sports game. We practised every Friday after school preparing for the inter-counties school competition. I was only a fair mid-field player and though small I was very fit and could run very fast with the ball on the stick. We had reached the Final and were to play Tullow in Carlow. I was very anxious about the game but my brothers kept encouraging me with their young expert advice.

The day of the Final came and we togged out. I arrived on the pitch – my heart was in my mouth! 'Would I be carried off in pain or what?' Well, my heart sank when I saw coming towards me my opposite number for the game. Oh, my God, but she was huge! 'She will murder me,' I thought She had these big broad shoulders, thick arms and trunks of legs. All of a sudden the whistle blew and the game was on. She pushed and shoved around trying to get possession of the ball. Our team had scored a few points. So far so good – in winning mode I thought. I was beginning to enjoy myself thinking your woman wasn't so bad after all. Half-time and we raced off to the sideline for a sip of orange juice, and off we went again into the second half.

My opponent now looked menacing very determined, dashing hither and thither, up and down the field with her hair and skirt flying. And then it happened. She gave me an almighty crack of her camogie stick on my shins – which sent me reeling onto the ground. I could see stars! And the pain! I lay slumped on the grass. I could hear my brothers cheering me on and shouting from the side-lines, 'Get up Maureen – go on, go on, your winning.' I wasn't going to be carried off the pitch injured. I was made of tough stuff and I would not let the side down So, I crawled to my feet and with my shins aching, I limped over and back and up and down. Though now I was trying not to get too close to your woman for another of her mighty wallops! And all of a sudden the final whistle blew. Game over. We had won. Oh, joy!

I have the greatest admiration for the wonderful camogie players of today. Watching the finals in Croke Park these times I often wonder is there anyone out there who have had their shins kicked and bruised and walloped like I had when I played the famous final all those years ago. I'm sure there are.

But I have to tell you that the Carlow Final was my last camogie game and, as they say, I've lived to tell the tale!

Maureen Maloney

The Upper Liffey

I was sixteen years old when I first cycled to Clocklea Bridge above Manor Kilbride. An old black heavy Raleigh bicycle was my transport and I had to push the pedals hard to ascend the "embankment" to Crooksling on the way. Strapped to the cross-bar, I had an old fly fishing rod, which had belonged to my father and I had his wicker creel on a leather strap around my shoulder,

At Clocklea was an old Church of Ireland building with a graveyard beside it. To guard against theft I would park my bike among the tombstones, hiding it from the road. And I felt very clever in the sunlight of day at having thought of such a ploy. Setting off along the Upper Liffey, rod held high, I leaped from rock to rock, all the while casting my flies for wild brown trout in the bog brown pools between. The place was enchanting, especially in May, when the bluebells in bloom mingled with the green ferns along the river bank. I thought of my fathers story, that he had once been accosted, on a bad fishing day, by the Reverend Rector of Clocklea Church, who stated that fish should not be caught on the Sabbath day on his stretch of water. My father, who was always good at turning a story his way, knew full well that it was Sunday, but was smarting from the effects of a blank day and an empty creel. 'Who is catching fish, anyway?' he purportedly growled at the Vicar.

When returning in the dark, I was suddenly terrified of walking into the Church yard to retrieve my bicycle. The bravado of the sunlit day was long gone as I searched around among the gravestones looking for my trusty steed. Everything seemed different at this time of night. A brush with a white cow that had wandered in across a broken stone wall put the heart crossways in me. Leaving the location in a hurry, I was soon bowling along on the bike, heading for Brittas. As I began the freewheel descent towards Tallaght, the vista of the lights of Dublin city spread before me and I savoured the moment. I felt the welcome weight of the trout in my creel and I knew that the little spotted beauties would do the showman in me no harm at all when I showed them to my father in the morning.

Paddy Conneff

Trains

I spent my early childhood on Moyne Road, Ranelagh. At the rear of the house ran what we called the Harcourt line. This was the railway that ran from Harcourt Street to Bray, passing through such exotic places as Dunville Avenue, Shankhil and Carrickmines. At first I remember the old steam trains.

As kids we used to amuse ourselves in winter, when snow fell, by pelting the passing carriages with snowballs. We were very close to the station and often were chased by an irritated station master. Once, he actually followed me home and as I hid in the bedroom, I could hear him complaining loudly to my father. There was also a foot bridge over the tracks, and another diversion we had was to make large snowballs and try to drop one down the funnel of passing trains. We thought that if our aim was good we could extinguish the fire and bring the train to a halt. Needless to say we never succeeded!

Another trick we had was to put the old halfpennies on the track letting the train run over them making them larger. Then, we would try to pass the flattened coin off for a full penny worth of sweets in the local shop. This shop was run by two old dears, whom we called the 'twits.' They were half blind and deaf and we hoped we could fool them with the flattened coins.

I don't know if anyone remembers the old 'stink bombs.' These were glass vials, which, when burst, gave off a vile smell of rotten eggs. I was to learn later in chemistry class in school that this was Sulphur Dioxide ($SO2$). So, frequently, we dropped these in their shop and watched hilariously from behind a hedge as they furiously tried to rid the shop of the stink.

The steam trains were eventually replaced by diesel engines, and the line was closed down by Todd Andrews, the then Minister for Transport.

The line lay derelict for many years but now I am happy to say it is used by the new LUAS trains, a great benefit to commuters.

Mike Mahon

The First Christmas I Remember

Phena and her two brothers

I love Christmas! This, I now know, goes back to the first Christmas I remember. I was almost five. My older brother, John, was almost seven and my baby brother Pat, was almost three. Just six months before this, on 3rd of July our mother had died.

I was alright about her dying as I knew she just flew up, up along our church steeple to heaven and was happily looking after us. It didn't matter to us too much as we had our Auntie Kathleen to mind us. She was my mother's youngest sister, pretty, fun and was our Christmas angel.

On Christmas Eve, there was spicy potato stuffing in a white basin ready to turn into dumplings next day. There was a big turf fire where a goose would be cooked in our biggest iron pot. The Tilly lamp was bright and we heard Santa read out our names on Radio Éireann. Bing Crosby sang 'I'm dreaming of a white Christmas.' Later, my father got a glass of Guinness from our pub across the street and a slice of porter cake was left on the table opposite the fireplace for Santa, and we went excitedly to bed.

Next morning at six, with flash lamp in hand, we clung to him going down the stairs. Santa had only left crumbs, but there were no presents around our big fireplace. We searched and found three wrapped boxes; behind the sofa, in the fire grate and a fourth at the chimney opening in our sitting room.

I got a rag doll, John a wooden building set and my baby brother a tin train and.... a packet of Woodbine cigarettes which thrilled him to bits – he being an occasional smoker at the tender age of four and a half !

Phena O'Boyle

All I Could See Was Larry

Eileen's Granddaughter

The love of my life was Larry. We had no money, but married and lived on true love. Very soon the babies arrived. We had two handsome boys and then two beautiful girls. Life was good but my happiness ended when my love died on 22nd May, 1983. My heart turned to stone and I was helpless as to how to deal with it.

Life goes on as it does and three years later I had a call from my son, Niall, to say Tina his wife had a baby and all were well. This was wonderful news and Niall collected me and couldn't contain his excitement when he brought me into the hospital to show off his daughter. I looked into the cot and the tears came to my eyes as I saw my beautiful granddaughter. She looked up at me with those dark eyes and all I could see was Larry.

This lovely baby was very special to me. She was wild and full of life; so bright and intelligent. This wonderful granddaughter, Kerrie, brought her grandmother into the 21st century. She taught me all about mobiles and computers; introduced me to all her friends. At twenty two, she has given me a lovely little great grandson.

Love never ceases. Love is life.

Eileen Williamson

A Final Resting Place

This year marks the 50th anniversary of the dedication of an unusual resting place.

You've probably passed it yourself on the road from Enniskerry to Glencree - a signpost points to a gate between two old lime trees. It reads: 'Deutscher Soldatenfriedhof - the German Military Cemetery'. Inside, the cemetery nestles in the palm of an old quarry, not a stone's throw from the Glencree Centre for Reconciliation. I was based in the Centre for a while and found myself drawn to this place from time to time.

I pieced together as much as I could about the history of the cemetery. I discovered that the German War Commission, with the help of the Irish Government, transferred the remains of German war dead there during the years 1959 and 1961. They considered it be a more dignified resting place and one that visitors could reach more easily.

Up to this the dead had lain buried near where they had died, or where locals had discovered their bodies, in different parts of mainland Ireland or on offshore islands.

Altogether in an exhaustive exercise, remains were exhumed from a total of 100 sites covering 15 different counties throughout the Republic. The cemetery was dedicated on 9th July 1961 and since then it has been looked after by the Irish government on behalf of the German War Graves Commission. There are 134 graves in the cemetery. Most are for Luftwaffe (air force) or Kriegsmarine (navy) personnel. Some of the deaths of German airmen killed in action over Ireland were caused by their aircraft getting lost in bad weather, or crashing as a result of damage in action over England. Others ran out of fuel or made navigational errors.

Alongside the airmen are a number of naval personnel whose bodies were found washed up on beaches around Ireland – sometimes in remote coastal locations. Probably the most unfortunate victims were forty six German civilian detainees who had been rounded up in Great Britain at the beginning of hostilities. By a cruel irony which often happens in wartime, these detainees along with a contingent of Italian detainees, were being shipped from England to Canada when their ship, 'The Andorra Star', was torpedoed by a German U-boat off Tory Island. This was in July 1940. Although civilians, the Andorra Star dead were deemed to be military casualties and so were entitled to be buried in the military cemetery. They were joined by six lone soldiers of the First World War who are also interred in the cemetery. These soldiers died while prisoners in a British prisoner of war camp located in Ireland in 1915/1918.

On my first visit to the cemetery I stopped to read the inscription on the three-faced stone standing beside the entrance. The words, translated into Irish, English and German, were written by Professor Stan O'Brien.
They read: *'What I dreamed and planned bound me to my fatherland, but war sent me to sleep in Glencree.'*

Just inside the entrance I passed a small Hall of Honour. Its interior is decorated in gilded mosaics designed by Bere, the Munich painter. It features a pieta surrounded by inscriptions in German. At its foot lie remainders of recent official visits – a garland of olive leaves dressed with black and yellow German ribbons and, as somewhat as a surprise to me, two poppy wreaths laid by the British Legion.

Among dwarf heather shrubs, carved granite crosses are grouped in pairs. Neat lines of granite headstones lying flat bear the dates of births and death of the two dead lying beneath them. As I walked around the paths between the headstones, I couldn't help but observe with sadness that so many of the fallen had died in their teens and twenties.

In the far right of the cemetery, against the rock face of the quarry, I was surprised to find the only upright headstone. It is a fine stone with a broadsword carved in relief and entwined in vines and thorns. I since discovered that it is believed to have been carved by the man who lies nearby when he was interred in the Curragh – Dr Herman Goertz, a convicted German spy.

As children, we used to run past his house on the Templeogue Road, and in hushed tones we pointed it out to others as the German spy's home.

He was paroled in 1947 and was informed he would be deported to Germany. Terrified that he would be handed over to the Soviets, he swallowed a cyanide capsule. He died at Mercer's Hospital soon after. His remains were buried in Deansgrange Cemetery in May 1947, his coffin draped in the Swastika flag. There they reposed until April 1974, when under the cover of darkness, some German ex-army personnel exhumed his body and interred him in the Glencree cemetery where he remains to this day.

Of the 81 Luftwaffe and Kreigsmarine buried in Glencree 53 are identified, 28 are unknown. The unknown are indicated by the poignant words: 'Zwei Deutsche Soldaten' – Two German Soldiers or 'Ein Deutsche Kreigstater' – Two German War dead.

On my most recent visit to the cemetery, it occurred to me how appropriate it is that these young victims of war should be resting close to the Glencree Centre for Peace and Reconciliation.

As I stood alone in silent prayer, I felt enveloped by a strange melancholy. Beneath me rows of young men far from home lay waiting, waiting, in the hush. At least it seemed to me to be a hush until I suddenly became aware of a robin bursting his red breast in song and the brown and white water laughing its way through moss and stone to the mouth of the valley below.

Rick Quinn

Dr. Goertz's house in Templeogue.

Hospital Days

The noise was terrible. The old man was brought wrestling and shouting into the ward. He had been in a fight in the Iveagh Hostel and claimed that both his legs were broken. Not bad for an eighty year old. Somebody had been thrown down the stairs, they said. It must have been him. He resisted all attempts by the nurses to undress him. 'We have to give you a bath, Sir,' said Julie, the staff nurse. There was a long pause. Then, 'Oh shame on you! Shame on you! And I thought you were a nice girl,' said the auld guy. At which point, patience having run out, he received a jab with a needle, which knocked him out.

When Old Peter woke up in the bed later that night, spic and span and bathed he changed tack completely. Although still noisy, he had now become intent on inviting the nurse who had performed the washing, into the bed with him. She had become the object of his fondness.

This happened in the old St. Vincent's Hospital at Stephens Green, where I was lying in the accident ward on a boarded bed. It had been the only bed available when I was taken in as an urgent case. Only the day before, I had undergone three and a half hours of surgery on my left inner ear. Now I had a head like a trussed up chicken, with my one good ear protruding and my bloodshot eyes glowering out from under a fringe of white muslin. Recently engaged to Rosemarie, my friends were totally convinced that it was only because I had become seriously ill that I had decided to go straight and succumb to marriage.

A different voice, then: 'Jaysus, it's well for that fella with the bandage around his ears,' came the Dublin accent from one of the other beds. 'Will yer man never bloody well shut up? We can't get a wink of sleep.' Then, silence for a while. Some snoring. Just after that, a moan came from another direction. This time, nearer. It was the fella in the bed beside me, actually.

'Oh! dear God how did this ever happen to me? I've led a good life, said my prayers regularly and always kept myself scrupulously clean.'

This poor man, it turned out had a boil, on a very private part of his body. 'Ha. Ha. Ha! We know what happened, don't we lads?' came a chirpy young voice from the bed over in the corner. 'Too much hurlin', that's what causes it. You holy fellas can't be trusted, you know. Ha, Ha, Ha. Sure you're always at it.'

Indeed, the man's holiness had been in evidence only the night before. A picture on the wall in front of us was askew, probably knocked accidentally out of kilter by a hospital cleaner. 'That thing is driving me mad,' I had said through my pain. Upon hearing this, 'Holy Joe' beside me, decided that I was an atheist, and that it was the subject matter of the nuns' holy picture that I was objecting to, not its crooked position on the wall. So he had pleaded, successfully as it turned out, with the nurses to have the lights put out ten minutes early, so that prayers in the shape of the Holy Rosary could be offered up for my redemption. Dear Lord, preserve us! Sure the poor girls were only too delighted to plunge us into darkness a little earlier than usual and go down to their station for a much needed cup of tea.

But I did have a favourite guy in the ward. Jem, a tough leathery man from Carlow had his car parked just outside our window in the doctors reserved space. 'I'm going home tomorrow,' he said. 'You can't,' I said. 'They won't give you your clothes. And they won't let you drive.' 'What they don't know won't hurt them,' said Jem. 'What was wrong with you anyway?', came another voice. Jem vaguely indicated his belly. 'What did you have done to you? Did you have an incision? How did you know in the first place?' The questions came from the men. The country man puckered up one eye and then looked knowingly through the other. 'It was the Vet that first put me wise,' he said.

The next day a loud argument could be heard with doctors and nurses as Jem requested his clothes. Eventually, then: 'Well OK so, but you'll have to sign yourself out. We are not taking responsibility.' Jem complied, and we watched through the window as his old mud spattered car turned out of the doctor's car park and pointed towards the country.

My pal was gone. But I had to wait another two weeks for my own freedom. 'At least I should be able to walk now without leaning over like the tower of Pisa,' I consoled myself.

Paddy Conneff

Love Knows No Bounds

Pauline and the boss's son

I first set eyes on him when he called to my workplace on an errand and my two immediate thoughts were – he's rather dishy and I would like to see and know more about him. Being quite crafty and scheming, I arranged for him to be invited to a charity event which I would be attending shortly thereafter. My plans worked out perfectly and we hit it off right away and arranged to meet again the following week. Our relationship thrived and soon we were meeting on a regular basis and a strong bond was developing between us.

However, looking ahead, I foresaw a problem down the line if we were to continue meeting. You see, my beau was the son of my boss and I seriously worried about how our relationship would be perceived – not just by my boss but also by my work colleagues. The expression 'love knows no bounds' proved true as our perseverance ensured that all the obstacles were overcome; not alone did I enjoy the warm support of my colleagues but I was welcomed with love and affection into what was to become my new family and soon we were discussing wedding plans. Now, almost forty four years later, I look back with fondness and gratitude at this happy and life-changing period of my life.

Pauline Doyle

St. Enda's Park

Bust of Pádraic Pearse in St Enda's Park

To arrive at Saint Enda's Park in the southern outskirts of Dublin is to arrive at a garden of green with a backdrop of the Dublin mountains. The grounds slope and drop away to the western side. From one of the walks I could look down on a small lake and hear the splashing of a small waterfall. Although it was early March there was the promise of spring flowers. The trees were mature as might be expected as the house was of the Georgian Period having been built in 1780. The house was the home of Pádraic Pearse who went to live there when he was 31 years old. That was about one hundred years ago when the house and grounds were in the country and the air was clean and fresh.

Pádraic had studied languages and had qualified as a barrister. He had founded a successful school in Ranelagh for boys but decided that the house in Rathfarnham was more suitable. He had an enlightened and humanitarian view of education. Corporal punishment was kept to a minimum. The curriculum included art and the natural sciences as well as languages such as English and French and his great love, Irish which he was very keen to conserve. The garden and grounds would have been ideal for nature study. His love of nature was obvious from his poem 'The Wayfarer' in which he writes,

'Sometimes my heart hath shaken with great joy
To see a leaping squirrel in a tree,
Or a red ladybird upon a stalk,
Or little rabbits in a field at evening.'

Pádraic was a visionary and hoped for an Ireland free from British rule. He wrote a poem entitled 'The Fool' which I think shows that he knew people would not understand him and what he yearned for. The following is an extract.

'Since the wise men have not spoken, I speak that am only a fool;
A fool that hath loved his folly,
Yea, more than the wise men their books, or their counting houses or their quiet homes,
Or their fame in men's mouths;
A fool that in all his days hath done never a prudent thing,
Never hath counted the cost, nor recked if another reaped
The fruit of his mighty sowing; content to scatter the seed;
A fool that is unrepentant, and that soon at the end of all
Shall laugh in his lonely heart as the ripe ears fall to the reaping- hooks
And the poor are filled that were empty,
Tho' he go hungry.
I have squandered the splendid years that the good God gave to my youth
In attempting impossible things, deeming them alone worth the toil.'

While I like Saint Enda's Park, the execution by firing squad in 1916 of the talented young man who lived there will always hang over it like a dark cloud.

Opal Peard

The Phone

I n the fifties we had the big heavy black phone. It had the finger dialling and a ring that sounded like the Fire brigade. Then in the sixties we had the American influence with plenty of colour and the button dialling. The little phone seat in the hall was very popular in the sixties. My refuge was to sit there talking to my friends with a cup of coffee and a cigarette, away from the madding crown in the kitchen. Another improvement was the cordless phone, which allowed you to walk up and down while you talked.

And yet again in the eighties came the mobile phone. It is hard to believe that such a tiny phone smaller than a packet of cigarettes could record so much information. My whole every day life is in that mobile. It comes everywhere with me, even to bed, and in the morning gives me a nice little reminder of what I have to do that particular day. The children as young as twelve have phones today. This is good, as it gives them security and keeps them in touch with home which is very comforting to the parents. The older children don't want to be in touch and never have any credit so if you want to get in touch with them just ring, don't text. It is a most wonderful invention and it can be used in detective work and the signal can pinpoint the exact location. Many murders have been solved through the mobile. A few years ago two mountaineers in Kerry, who got into difficulty, were rescued and brought to safety as a direct result of their signal in their mobile phones.

Eileen Williamson

First Love

Three pals in Coláiste Pádraig

I think it was the golden crest on his navy blue blazer! It dazzled me. Then I noted his wavy blonde hair, his blue eyes and fair complexion.

It was our first morning at Coláiste Pádraig in Spiddal, Co.Galway in 1965. I and my two pals, Anne and Monica were with me there to learn to speak Irish for our Leaving Cert and we were sixteen and full of joy. Anne's mother and gran, both teachers, were our minders for the week and their caravan was our holiday home!

On the very first night we went to the 'Halla Mór' for my very first céile and I didn't dare look towards this blonde Adonis. With girls on one side and boys on the other, it was a frightening moment. Would he notice all those beautiful girls who gave the glad eye or was there a chance that I might be picked? Well glad to tell you I was. We didn't talk any English and Irish meant very few words were said, but none were needed....We danced the siege of Ennis, reels and jigs but most of all we danced the last dance. My friends, Anne and Mon didn't exist; I was in another place and mere mortals couldn't get there! He walked me home along Galway bay, as Anne and Mon followed close behind us - in order to watch every move, but it didn't matter as we just held hands on every night as we walked from the 'Halla Mór' to our caravan on Spiddal's shore.

I lost my appetite, however and Anne's mother got really worried. I couldn't eat as the pain in my heart was all-consuming and the food of first love was enough for me!

Phena O'Boyle

On Leaving Home

I was just 18 when I first left home. My mother thought I had the makings of a teacher but I wanted to be a bookkeeper. So arrangements were made for me to go to Dublin to commence a commercial course and stay with my cousin in Killester. My mother had lovingly packed my bag and my father had rummaged in his wallet for a pound note to give me – a sort of fortune then.

The bus stopped opposite the Gárda Station where I had lived for 10 years. I hugged and cried as I left my good parents and sitting in a window seat so that I could have a last long look at them and the village that I loved. My cousin met me in Dublin that Friday evening. My course started at the College on the following Monday. I was so excited, making sure I got there in good time to find my class-room for my first lesson of the day, which was Gregg's Shorthand.

I decided to sit in a front row desk, as I was small. There was plenty of chatter going on while all eagerly awaiting the arrival of the teacher, a Miss O'Connell. All of a sudden the door burst open and in walked this large woman clad in a flowing black gown. My heart sank straight away, remembering the gentle entrance of the nuns I had as teachers, and their demeanour in the class-room.

'Let's begin,' Miss O'Connell said, eyeing each one of us critically. She called out our names and ticked them off in her long ledger. And thus began for me the first most horrible lesson of that 9-month shorthand course. I certainly did my best by constantly practising the outlines of the dictation that were given each day when I got back to my cousin's house. After a few weeks I was able to go home for a weekend. My mother was at the bus-stop and threw her arms around me in a loving embrace that I can feel still. I started to cry but said little of my torment.

Inside in the barrack kitchen my father and brothers all wanted to hear about my life in Dublin.

My mother had been a bookkeeper, and she was dying to hear all about the typing, and shorthand, and bookkeeping methods. I kept it all as light as I could – not telling them about the shorthand teacher' snide remarks, and calling on me to read back the piece of correspondence she had just dictated, at 60, 80 or 100 words per minute, saying 'We'll ask the Leaving Cert country girl to read first.' And I would begin, 'Dear Sir, we thank you for your letter of the 22nd , and so on.' Half-way down the passage the nerves would kick in and I would stumble and stutter over the part, where it was 'the engineer's supervisor' or was it 'the engineering supervision.' Knowing the whole class was listening to me, I could hear tittering at the back. Agonisingly, I would finish the piece and Miss O'Connell would say, 'Now we'll hear how it should be read. Judy, you'll show the Leaving Cert country girl how to read it.' And I would squirm with embarrassment in my seat.

At the end of my homely and enjoyable weekends, I would start to cry, not only because I was leaving my familiar home, parents and brothers, but because I had to face into shorthand class again to be humiliated by the now familiar call of Miss O'Connell: 'Let the Leaving Cert country girl start.' My parents never knew about any of this. In the culture of the time of over 50 years ago, what happened in the class-room stayed in the class-room. And to think that went on for me, week after week, for nine months until the exam in June. Had I told my father, as a Gárda Sergeant, I'm certain he would have made it his business to come up to town and confront Miss O'Connell.

When the results came out, from a class of twenty two I had secured first place in Commercial Arithmetic, third place in

Bookkeeping and fifth place in Business Methods. I was way down the list in shorthand and typing. Before I left the College that day, the Commerce Teacher called me aside. 'Tell me, Maureen, what happened in the shorthand and typing classes – you did so well in my classes – whatever was the cause?' she enquired gently. 'Well, Miss McCarthy,' I said, 'if I told you about your colleague, Miss O'Connell and how she behaved towards me all through the course you would not believe me. So leave it. It is too late now anyway.' She stared at me in astonishment and, yes, pity. She had been so nice and gentle to me and she herself was an excellent teacher. I always remembered her with affection but I will never forget the look on her face that day. 'Why didn't you come to me?' she said.

I got my first job almost immediately as a junior bookkeeper in a large firm in North Frederick Street. My mother was thrilled about it and I loved it, and it can be said I never looked back. Yet, when I think of those years, long ago, crying for joy when I went home to be received with such love and care, and crying when I was leaving. Not only because I was leaving my home and parents behind, but the thought of that Shorthand Teacher dragging me down. Leaving home – under such circumstances - was one of the hardest things I ever had to do........

Maureen Maloney

My Early Life

Farm Cart

About my early life, my memory, coming from a farming background, was planting the potatoes in Spring and going to the bog to wheel out the turf. The bog was about two miles from the house. I remember my Grandfather drawing a circle on the ground when the sun was shining. He would put all the figures of the clock from one to twelve; he would then put two sticks at the correct time. A shadow would form and show the time all through the day, so we would know when to have dinner - we would have tea and sandwiches at four o'clock.

In summer, we would go to the bog to save the turf. We would put it into reeks to dry. Another job was to save the hay. Great memories we had, good times and bad. We made our own fun. A gang of us would get together on Sunday and play football. On Sunday night, we would go to a film or dance. The next job was to save the corn. It would be put into big reeks in a garden for threshing. That day all the neighbours would gather in the garden. That night, there would be a meal for everyone afterwards with a few drinks and a sing song.

In winter, we would pick the potatoes and bring home the turf. A big reek would be made of the turf. We put the potatoes in the garden, covered them with straw and clay. Then we thatched them with straw on top. After all this work, we looked forward to Christmas. Christmas morning was a big surprise. Santa came with presents. On Stephen's Day we went to hunt the wren. That night we went to a dance to make a day and night of it.

Jim Browne

Brittas Bay

One of my abiding memories of childhood was the long summer days we spent in Brittas Bay. My Dad was in the building business and the traditional builders' holidays were the first two weeks of August. We were a family of five children, but had many aunts and uncles and myriads of cousins. As there was not enough room in the cars to transport us all to Brittas, my father got a long low loader truck, on which he built a frame and covered it over in canvas. It was like a large tent on wheels. The adults traveled by car, but all us kids were bundled into this contraption. We were delighted. We fitted it out with cushions, rugs, old car seats and beach towels and set off in convoy for Brittas Bay. Sometimes, there might have been ten or twelve of us plus a few dogs, but we thought the 'craic was mighty.'

The roads were not very good in those days, so there were frequent stops to repair punctures or overheating engines. We were like a small army on the move, the amount of paraphernalia we carried for the picnic. There were kettles, pots and pans, primus stoves, rugs, wind-breakers, table cloths, dishes, cutlery, billy cans, sun umbrellas, LILO's, deck chairs and even a few plastic blow-up crocodiles. Of course, the weather was not always favourable, and I can remember well Uncle Dick and Dad hunching out in the lashings of rain, furiously pumping the primus stoves, trying to boil water for tea, while we kids sat in our dry mobile tent munching sandwiches. Any time now I eat a tomato and cheese sandwich, I can still get the taste of sand in my mouth. One old aunt, Aunt Dolly, would bring a mountain of sandwiches of dubious ingredients, and when we inquired what was in them, she would dismiss us with a wave of her hand, ' They're et cetera sandwiches; what ever came to hand. Eat up and don't be cheeky.' I munched on what tasted like a cheese sandwich, only it had bones in it.

Regardless of the weather, us kids always managed to get into our togs for a swim, build sand castles or just muck about. Looking back on it now as an adult, it reminds me of some sort of medieval punishment. We were always blue, shivering with the cold, trying to dry ourselves with a wet towel or sheltering from the rain under a plastic Mac. Days later we would still be brushing sand from our cracks and crevices.

The journey back to Dublin was another adventure. It was usually late in the day and we usually stopped at one of the many pubs. Now in those days, children were not allowed into pubs. So, as the adults went in for 'a few jars', us kids were left to our own devices in our four wheeled tent. We were happy being kept well supplied with drinks of red lemonade and glasses of rasp-berry cordial. We would have already stocked up well with such goodies as gob stoppers, bulls eyes, liquorish-all-sorts, fizz bags, dolly mixtures, Marietta biscuits and slabs of gur cake, which was like dead flies between two pieces of pastry. Exhausted but happy we would eventually get home to Dublin and our proper beds.

Brittas Bay has changed a lot in the intervening years. Many of the beautiful beaches have been fenced off by land owners. Old country houses have been converted into luxury hotels, and spas and a spate of holiday homes were built during the boom.

Mike Mahon

Young Love

Behind the Backdrop

We are all together, young boys and girls in our early teens – we call ourselves the Barton Amateur Dramatic Society. I am tingling with excitement.

She is with me behind the backdrop - waiting to go on. Joyce O'Sullivan - a lovely girl from Dingle with a teasing accent, full of music.

I have a fierce crush on her. We are very aware of one another – alone behind the curtain. I see her lips moistening. I watch her young bosom rise and fall.

I am nearly passing out.

I feel all shy and yet I want to touch her.

We do not kiss.

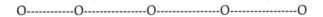

Fifty five years later, my brother and his wife were on a cruise on the Nile. They got talking to a couple who were also from Ireland.

When he said that he was a Quinn, originally from Barton in Rathfarnham, she asked if he was a brother of Rick? She laughed when she recalled that we had been members of the Bar-

ton Amateur Dramatic Society together. She didn't say any more
about us but revealed that her maiden name was Joyce O'Sulli-
van. My boyhood crush!

All these years later, was she remembering our brief en-
counter behind the curtain?

Rick Quinn

Amsterdam

DC3

J ust after getting my Commercial Pilot's Licence, I managed to get a job in Amsterdam. The company employed contract workers around Europe, who needed to travel to different locations, and to do this as cheaply as possible they procured a few clapped-out World War Two DC3's. The guy in charge of the flight operations was from Shannon and well known in Irish aviation circles; a very likeable wheeler dealer and con artist. When I arrived first to take up the job I would need an endorsement from their Aviation Authority, as the aircraft were Dutch registered. 'No problem,' Captain B informed me, took my Irish licence, stuffed a few bottles of Scotch in his briefcase and disappeared. Later that afternoon, he arrived back with my licence duly endorsed. This was to be the modus operandi for all our operations.

I was very new to the DC3. However, once airborne, B disappeared down the cabin and left me to my own devices in the cockpit. He would spend the entire flight flogging duty free booze, cigarettes, perfume, watches and anything else he could acquire cheaply, to the passengers. On many occasions, on final approach into a busy airport I had to insist he come back to the cockpit for landing. We night-stopped regularly in London and stayed in one of the top hotels. We never paid a red cent; B had deals going with the concierge. We would arrive by taxi with a few crates of booze, guaranteeing a luxurious weekend. I never found out how he managed to get through Her Majesty's customs; suffice to say we always parked the aircraft in the cargo area.

The DC3 was a tail dragger converted from the US Air force C47's and difficult to control on take off and landings, especially in strong cross wind conditions. It needed lot of rudder control with both feet. It was therefore to my great surprise when I was rostered to fly to Glasgow with a Dutch captain who had one leg shorter than the other. I don't know how he managed to get checked out on type. These aircraft were not pressurised, so we couldn't fly above 10,000 feet with passengers. This meant flying at lower altitudes and getting bumped all over the place in turbulent conditions. The rules of the air were not just bent but well a truly broken in the interests of Mammon. Fortunately, I did not have to stay in this job too long and lost touch with Captain B.

Some years later his photograph appeared on the front page of one of the redtops. He was pictured standing in front of an English stately mansion, with a Rolls Royce in the background. He was proclaimed to be an entrepreneur selling villas in Spain to retired couples. I was not surprised to learn later on that he was serving a jail sentence for fraud.

Mike Mahon

Working in Canada

Canadian Mounties

I started my working life as an office boy during the last world war but quickly moved on to other things, eventually becoming a sales rep in the clothing trade.

A big change occurred when in the early fifties I, with my wife and family, went to live in Toronto, Canada. At that time Toronto was a fast growing city and I went to work for the Singer Company, a large and diverse company, which had many retail stores throughout Canada. After a couple of years, I became manager of the main store in downtown Toronto.

Part of my duties was to hire and train people to work in the store. One of these was a lady named Clare, all the way from Wicklow Town. Part of the service we provided was to make buttonholes for customers who made their own garments. Clare came to my office one day because a customer had brought back a garment, which she claimed wasn't wearable, due to a mistake in making the buttonholes. We should make a refund of $10, which she claimed the garment was worth. Clare said the garment wasn't even worth $5. I spoke to the customer briefly and promptly made a refund of the full $10. End of story? No.

About six months later, I was asked to come to the shop floor to see a young couple who wanted to buy a sewing machine. I demonstrated and sold our top of the line model. After the sale, I enquired as to why they had asked for me to look after them. The young lady explained what had happened about the prompt refund six months previously. That was the reason for the purchase.

As I explained to Clare later, the 'customer is always right.'

Albert Connor

Running The Mile For Synge Street

Synge Street CBS Crest

I t was the Iveagh Grounds. The mile race started to an ear-splitting noise as the boys stamped in the stand and roared on their school runner. The man with the starting gun was Bobby Payne, who snarled the starting orders in a way that would have unsettled nerves of steel.

Dermot Gygax of O'Connell's Schools immediately took the lead and strode away. Knowing nothing else, I gave a little sprint and tucked in behind him. Together, we moved away and soon there was an enormous gap from the rest. At the halfway mark, somebody shouted out: '2 minutes and 9 seconds.' I had surely blown it. This was faster than I had ever run a half mile race, much less the first half of the longer race. I would surely collapse. As we came towards the middle of the third lap, my legs were on fire. It was taking three times the effort to keep going.

Out of the corner of my eye, I could see 'Jiggers', our Christian Brother coach, towel in hand. He turned his head. 'Jesus, Mary and Joseph,' he bellowed; 'is that Paddy Conneff up there at the front? Come on Paddy. Come on Paddy.' We were past him then and I yearned for the bell.

Suddenly, there was a loud clang and we were on the last lap. I was still hanging onto Gygax's shoulder and thinking of how I would get past him. The burning fire had gone and my legs were as cold as ice, but still moving. Lactic acid was paralysing my muscles as Gygax moved three yards away from me.

I went to follow but was not quick enough. The early pace had told. We had slowed down and some of the pursuing athletes had closed on us. Blackrock and Clongowes had managed to insert themselves between me and the leader with only 300 yards to go. I was the fastest sprinter left in the shake-up, but I was blocked. I sensed my mistake and dropped back to run around the outside. I took out after the leader, but it was too late. We both finished in 4 minutes and 50 seconds with Dermot Gygax a fraction in front. I was to discover later that the Leinster Schools record for the mile was held at the time by an ex-Synge Street boy called Ryan, at 4 minutes and 49 seconds.

I stood beside the finish and relished the cessation of effort. After a while, I decided to walk towards my tracksuit, which was lying only a few yards away but my feet seemed stuck to the ground. I fell over, and it took the St. Johns Ambulance lads some time to revive me.

For me there was now relief and some disappointment. A sense of what might have been. But a second place medal was not the worst and would help the school team.

Paddy Conneff

Growing Up In Roscommon

Kevin (on left) and siblings in Roscommon

I grew up on a small but fertile farm in Clooneyquinn, County Roscommon, in the late Thirties and early Forties. My earliest memories are mostly of wonder and magic, though there were some tears. Let me share my memories with you.

When I was very young I remember my Dad taking me with him out in the field. He'd spread out his large heavy overcoat, wrap me in it and I'd have a good sleep while he worked. Later I remember running barefoot in the meadow, catching butterflies and bees or searching for wild birds' nests. In those days too, I learned how to fish.

Every season brought a new wonder and magic. In springtime I'd watch the hen laying and hatching her eggs. I loved the way she cared for her chicks and nursed them under her wing. How could I forget the wonder of wild flowers and the hawthorn bush in summer? Then later on I remember shaking the plum tree till the lovely ripe plums fell at my feet
and picking the biggest juiciest apple in our own little orchard.

Let me finish by remembering the wonderful people who reared me and cared for me. May they reap their just reward!

Kevin McGrath

Love In A Lab

Zoology Department TCD

T here was an envelope in my cubby hole. With my heart beating a little quicker, I withdrew it. It was indeed a Valentine card. Inside the card was sketched a self portrait in profile and it was initialled. The distinctive triangular nose left no doubt as to the identity of the sender.

It was the culmination of a growing attraction which had blossomed as the weeks went by. As students in Trinity College, Dublin, we had found ourselves side by side during Zoology practical work, where wearing our white laboratory coats we would try to dissect a worm or a frog or some other specimen before lunch. From time to time we would glance up from our work and smile at one another. Our glances became gazes until eventually our eyes became locked and all else faded away. Our teacher would quietly call us back to the work at hand.

We met for afternoon tea at the Metropole Cinema near Nelson Pillar. 'What happened after that?' enquired my daughter. 'Oh, it was all downhill from then on. I was overcome with shyness and walked into the glass door. I became tongue-tied and couldn't think of anything to say. I lost my fragile composure entirely and I had forgotten my handkerchief. Not surprisingly, it was the end of this affair. The Easter Holidays intervened. When the new term resumed, I returned the handkerchief I had borrowed. We never arranged another date. In fact, I hardly saw him again, even in the distance. Our timetables must have been different. Looking back, I realise I hardly knew him.'

'Did you tell Dad ever?' my daughter asked.

'Indeed, yes. I told him last night.'

'What!' she exclaimed. 'Fifty years later!!'

Opal Peard

The Terenure Enterprise Centre & Me

Pauline outside the Terenure Enterprise Centre in the early days.

U p to 1984, I had many varied and interesting work experiences. In fact, as already mentioned, I met my husband while in one particular job. However, I could not have foreseen that my next assignment would take me up to retirement age and also prove to be the most rewarding and fulfilling life event, outside of my family.

You see, early in 1984 I got involved in a community initiative in Terenure which had been set up in response to the serious economic recession which was then in Ireland. Not one to do things in half measures, I threw myself wholeheartedly into establishing the local community enterprise centre in my area, which it was hoped would provide work and training opportunities for many of the locally unemployed people. The initiative went from strength to strength and, today, the Terenure Enterprise Centre is recognised as a major success in the field of community development. I was fortunate to be among the driving forces of the organisation and happily remained in this position until my recent natural retirement.

My involvement however still continues today as, now, I find myself availing of the services of this same enterprise centre through many of the programmes offered specifically for local senior citizens.

Truly, I am reaping what I helped to sow; can I ask for more than this?

Pauline Doyle

Jack Switzer

Budding angler at Orwell

J ack Switzer was known as 'The Father of the Dodder.' He lived in the Lodge, Stratford Road, Rathgar. It was 1950 and the Dodder Anglers' Club, eventually to be famous, had not yet been founded. But Jack was already a well known sportsman and one of the oldest anglers on the river.

Jack would hold court at Orwell, Rathfarnham and Milltown, surrounded by young people, most of them budding anglers. He would talk of the fish in the Dodder. There were the trout, of course, but also the minnow, the stoneloach, the stickleback (we called them pinkeens or red breasters), the eels and the crayfish. For Jack however, the wild brown trout was king and he left us youngsters in no doubt at all about that.

Jack himself could lay claim to having captured a spotted beauty of five and a half pounds weight in the flat pool between Pearse Bridge and the Rathfarnham waterfall. He believed that in the winter floods, the big fish had been washed out of the Glenasmole reservoirs and down into the Dodder below.

The Glenasmole/Bohernabreena reservoirs formed the old Rathmines/ Rathgar water supply, and were known to us then simply as 'the waterworks.' The 'waterworks' held a wild brown trout population, which had been augmented with the famous

Loch Leven strain of trout from Scotland. This, it was believed, had added to the fighting qualities of the fish in the whole catchment. For Loch Leven was famous, and its trout had been stocked in lakes all over the world by the British, even as far away as the Himalayas.

Jack Switzer was a crack shot and had a .22 rifle which he had used for 55 years. He rode an old BSA two stroke motorbike, on which he would travel from Rathgar to the river. In the back satchel of the bike he had a Ludo board and would regularly challenge the young anglers to a game. He was also a veteran of the Battle of the Somme and readily told stories of the trenches to his assembled youngster audience. This audience included Rory Harkin, Sean Scully, Paddy Conneff, Joe McCarthy and Eddie Edmonds. Coincidentally, Eddie's own father, Samuel Edmonds, had also served at the Somme.

At the battle of the Somme, we were told Jack Switzer and Samuel Edmonds had differing roles. Jack had helped to man the trenches, his job being to shoot straight and try to stay alive. Sam on the other hand and his mates attended the gun carriages. Each carriage carried artillery and was drawn by a team of six horses. When an unfortunate animal or two went down under gunfire, Sam's men were there to get the dead horses unyoked and send the carriage with cannon on its way to make the best of it with what was left. Both Jack and Sam would tell of the temporary cessation of fighting which would take place from both sets of trenches when the world war one aeroplanes darkened the skies on high. Then the occupants of both the Allied and German trenches engaged in an impromptu ceasefire in order to watch the aerial combat unfolding high over their heads.

An abiding memory of Jack Switzer is of a sunny day and he standing below Orwell Bridge, his fishing rod propped against the stone wall, his fishing companion, John Dillon, standing beside him. To the assembled youngsters - trout fishing converts or addicts like himself - he was recounting a tale of the trenches. 'The shells were bursting in the water,' he said, 'and the fish were coming up dead.' There was a sustained 'ah' from the assembled boys, and we all went quiet.

Eventually Jack broke the silence. 'It was OK lads,' he said, 'the fish were only roach, auld coarse fish, an odd pike maybe, but no trout. There were no dead trout, lads.' The mood lightened immediately and the sun seemed to shine brighter.

Jack smiled through his silver military moustache and walked over to the stone wall of the river. He reached for his rod, made some adjustments to his cast and continued his fishing.

Paddy Conneff

Margaret

To me love is a long, loving relationship between two people.

When I was 16 and picking potatoes with my uncle a local girl, Margaret, was helping out that day. When the day's work was done and I was going home, my uncle called me and asked me to leave the girl home. She was 15, so we set out for home across the fields. When we came to the bushy gap the two of us climbed up on it. I got down the other side, Margaret asked me to lift her down. So, I did and that's when young love began.

We walked home through the fields, hand in hand, and there were a few kisses and cuddles. I remember that night we made a date to go to a film in a cinema in a local town. We went to films for about three months.

A carnival came to the town for two weeks. We went to it about for six nights. I remember there were bumper cars, swinging boats and chair planes that went fast around in a ring. All the big bands came to the carnival: Big Tom, Joe Dolan, the Premier Aces and Ray Lynam. We went to dances after the carnival. Then we went to films every Sunday night. We got very close and had some great times. As there was no work around, I had to go to the big lights of London.

I met Margaret when I was home on holidays and we kept in touch by letter. Then as time went on and we were apart for periods, we both met someone else and formed other relationships. But as Margaret and I came from the same area, we stayed friends.

Jim Browne

Grandad

Grandchildren

As I grow older, I'm happy that I'm still able to take on different interests and challenges. But nothing gives me greater pleasure than the time I spend with my young grandchildren, like the following afternoon on Greystones beach:

We walk across the grey stones to the water's edge. You see the waves creeping towards us in line after line with a swishing sound. You grasp my hand and then strangely you hesitate. The stones you had gathered to throw into the water you hold in your left hand and pass them to me with your right hand to throw them on your behalf. You shout with joy as you see the white plumes of water splash into the air.

'More' ...... 'More', you shout.

What thoughts are going through your young head? What little fears had made you hesitate?

You might have seen us on Greystones beach – a white haired man holding his two-year-old grandson's hand – the boy's golden curls shining like a monstrance in the evening sun.

A magic moment for me. The first of many more to come, I hope.

The future belongs to this generation. I just want to share some of it with them.

Rick Quinn

A Memory Of Schooldays

"There was an accident in school today, Mammy, and I did it!'

That statement of mine has followed me all my life from childhood.

I broke a glass vase in primary school in Kildare and my brothers have never let me forget it! It happened in 5th class. My pals and I would stay back to 'tidy up' the classroom. One day, just for fun when the nun had left the room, I fired a duster at my pal, Claire, and missed, hitting the glass vase on the little altar. It came crashing down smashing into smithereens. I nearly died! The nun came in just then. 'Who did this,' she asked. 'I did it, Sister,' I said. 'You'll have to replace it tomorrow, Maureen,' she said in a terrifying tone. Going home, I wondered how I would tell my mother. 'It was an accident,' I kept telling myself. 'It was just an accident.' We lived in Kildare town where my father was the Gárda Sergeant. What would he say when he heard my story?

At dinner my mother enquired, as she always did. 'How were things at school today then?' A lump came to my throat as I thought, 'How am I going to tell her and what about the expense of buying a new vase.' Just then my brothers came in. Immediately, I blurted out: 'There was an accident in school today and I did it.' All chorused just what I had said and danced around the kitchen with glee. My mother tried to control them. They kept it up and indeed for the rest of my young life. My father gave me the money for a cut-glass vase to present to the nun. After that incident I have rarely broken anything in my whole life.. A childhood lesson learned, indeed!!

Maureen Maloney

I Came To Dublin

A Delivery Man

Growing up on a farm in Clooneyquinn, County Roscommon was very good training for my first job.

In 1955 when I was 19 years of age I came to Dublin to look for work. My first job was delivering bread and cakes for Johnston, Mooney & O'Brien's Bakery, with a horse drawn van. I had no difficulty working a horse and taking care of him, as I was used to working horses on the farm. After some years, the horses gave way to motorised vans. I was employed with that company for 32 years.

My next job was a financial adviser for an insurance company. I worked for this Company for 15 years. I love gardening and worked at garden maintenance also. I was very lucky to have never been out of work during my working life.

Now it is great to be up early in the morning and not to have to hurry off to work.

Kevin McGrath

My Brother

My brother Paddy was nine years older than myself, and left me at a considerable loss when he joined the Defence Forces at age seventeen during the 1940 National Emergency, and was tragically killed in an accident shortly afterwards during training on explosives. However, during a few years before his departure, I was old enough to pick his brains on several matters needing to be sorted out by me on my early growth path. In our rural environment, there were, first of all, matters agricultural, involving donkeys and potatoes and turf-fuel and hay. Being a lot nearer to me in age than our father, it was natural that Paddy would be the first to consult for information or know-how, rather than Dad.

Donkeys were for farm-work, and needed to be properly used, so carts and creels and other gear must be attached in the right way, and the animal treated kindly. Potatoes were a chapter in themselves, not forgetting the cold task of bringing some home from a distant pit in frosty weather. The turf was a seasonal affair, started by digging out the peat in May or June, and getting it gradually dried out, before stacking it on the road-side for taking home by cart or lorry. The hay involved much more than 'casadh an t-sugáin' (twisting the hay-rope), from cutting to cocks, to bringing home on a hay-float and stacking or putting in a hay-shed. So much for farm-work.

I needed advice on the local fairies. What happened to Johnny Mac was a caution against being too greedy for work, rather than taking it in moderation. Johnny was so fit and well on one evening in early May, with a full moon just coming up, that he decided to continue cutting turf-sods by moon-light for a further while. He was alone, on the bog right on the top of Mullaghnashee and near the rockpile which gives the hilltop its name.

This means 'Summit of the fairy mound', and that mound of piled-up giant boulders might be the work of the fairies, or might be the outcome of ancient ice-sheets moving and thawing, conflicting views that need cause us no worry.

A little after moonrise, Johnny became aware the he was among a dozen little men in hard hats, dark swallow-tail coats and stout boots. One shouted 'Sir, if you cut them, we will spread them for you.' More than delighted to be saved the work of spreading out the sods for drying by using his wheelbarrow, Johnny cut the peat sods feverishly for a long time, while his little helpers spread them by hand. Finally, he collapsed in exhaustion onto a heathery bank nearby and fell asleep. When he awoke, it was daylight. He was surrounded by a large circular mound of fresh turf-sods, all needing to be spread by himself or other humans. Not a sod of the fairy spreading remained where he thought he saw them putting it.

Another neighbour, Matt, had a fairy encounter on the mountain, of a more subtle kind. In the dusk of a summer evening while coming back down from work on his turf, he found himself somehow astray, in a small field surrounded by a dense high thorn hedge which showed no gap or gate anywhere. Matt realised what might be at work and knew what to do. He took off his coat, turned it inside out, and then put it back on. The spell was broken, and he had no trouble finding his way out of the field and going on home. My brother Paddy warned me that small boys should not be alone on the mountain at night fall, and their wandering around should be done in broad daylight.

The leprechaun is a tricky lad, very hard to see. We hear him often enough, tapping away at the shoes, under some distant hawthorn. But he almost always notices our attempt to get a closer look, and what we see at shorter range is a thrush banging a snail-shell against a stone, an example of a bird using a tool, something birds are not supposed to do. Paddy was inclined to doubt whether the bird was real or not. I myself was also in two minds on this matter. Paddy sometimes passed me a cigarette, although I was so young, and as he and I smoked our thoughtful cigarettes.

They shed no further light on the mystery.

Eamon Henry

Rationing

I remember, during 'The Emergency', rationing took place and gas was one of the commodities in short supply, so at certain times in the day the pressure was reduced. The gas for technical reasons was never totally cut off, so a glimmer remained which could be used to heat milk or to slow cook. It was illegal to use the glimmer so an inspector, known as the 'Glimmer Man', was employed to call to houses to gain entry and inspect the hob. If it was warm to the touch the housewife was in trouble. The way out of this was to have a bucket of cold water at the ready to plunge the hot trivets into. These were the removable parts of the cooker. How well this system worked I don't know. I do remember the panic a knock at the door could induce.

My Mother decided to be very civic minded and to do her bit to save gas. She went to the library and found a book on making a hay box. She found a big wooden box probably a tea box. This was difficult to find during the war. The next thing was to find hay. I think she may have been given a bag of hay by a kindly bread delivery man who would have had a nose bag for his horse. She made a nest of hay in the box several inches thick to encompass a saucepan. The method of use was to bring a pot of porridge, for example, to the boil on the hob and then put it into the hay box covering the top with a pad of hay and leaving it overnight. In the morning the porridge would be cooked through requiring perhaps only a little reheating. A stew could be left all day. She also set up a cooking system using primus stoves. Somehow she had paraffin oil and a tiny bottle of methylated spirits as a primer. She felt very pleased about all this in spite of the inconvenience until one day there was a knock at the door. Outside were two gas men. 'We've come to put in a new gas meter, Missus.

The old one is not registering any gas usage.'

Opal Peard

The Land Commission

The Merrion Hotel (formerly the Land Commission)

When I left school I was encouraged to do the Civil Service Examination for Shorthand Typing. Then one day I got my letter to go for my Irish Oral Interview and after that a Medical Examination.

I was on my way to be a Civil Servant Typist. I started in the Land Commission at 24 Upper Merrion Street. There was a big bicycle shed at the back. Everybody used bicycles in the fifties. We then had to walk a very long corridor and up the stairs to the top of the house. The supervisor was there with the red pen if you were late. We often took the stairs in threes to sign before the red pen was drawn.

I was given a desk and typewriter in a room with ten other girls. There was a pot bellied stove to heat the room. It usually smouldered with wet turf and when anyone came in or out there was a billow of smoke into the room. The typewriters were Remington and very heavy and with ten going together they made a terrible racket. The girls were from every part of Ireland. Some found it very hard to manage as they had to pay for digs and food. The Dublin girls were a little better off if they lived at home. Despite this we had good fun and didn't seem to be affected too much.

There was a rule in the Civil Service that when women got married they had to leave work. This was revoked in 1973. As I got married before that time I was required to leave. Little did I know as I made my speech at my presentation that I would be back 26 years later.

That is a story for another day.

Eileen Williamson

The Holidays

The bus left Aston Quay for Kilkenny each evening at six o'clock in those days. Every summer of my childhood, we made the holiday trip 'home', as mother called it for all of her sixty years in Dublin. Some years we arrived far too early for the bus and if the rain was falling we crowded into McBirneys for shelter. The best way to describe this store was that it was a country cousin of Clerys in O'Connell Street. I still remember the uneven floors and the steps up and down to all the different departments. Going back in time, there were actually shoppers from various parts of the country who alighted from the buses in the morning, did their shopping there and returned home in the evening without ever crossing O'Connell Bridge.

When our bus eventually pulled in, we all piled on. Along with the passengers who boarded, many parcels and packages were also put on for delivery along the way. The first stop en route was early enough, at the Hideout in Kilcullen. Most of the adults alighted for 'refreshments.' Mother and Dad also went in, with many exhortations to the six of us children to be good. 'If you behave we'll have a treat when the bus restarts,' they promised. Anne the eldest of the family was left in charge and made very sure to keep order. They always came back in great form, a little bit fuzzy and slightly flushed - from all the rushing about they explained. Dad carried the Cleeves toffees and hard boiled sweets and mother held a large bottle of T.K Lemonade and paper cups. We knew the holidays had begun.

Pat Crotty, the driver, got back into his seat and with only a few brief stops to drop off the bundles of late final Evening Heralds along the way, we very soon reached our destination. Uncle Michael met the bus in Castlecomer as he did every evening, to collect his news papers and various other parcels and packets from the wholesalers in Dublin for his shop in the town. Auntie

Bridie was close on his heels with arms outstretched and smiling face, 'you are all so welcome to Comer,' she declared. 'Hurry along now as fast as you can. We have supper waiting below in the house and the children can't wait to see all of you young people.'

This was the start of our month's stay in the country.

Fia Weber

Birr Castle Demesne Visit

3rd Earl of Rosse's (Williams Parsons) Telescope

A visit to Birr Castle Demesne in County Offaly was made on Saturday 9 July 2011 by eleven members of the Active IT Society (AITS), organised and led by Mrs Angela Hickey. A two-hour journey by car got us there about noon, and after a light snack in the coffee-shop we started our tour, for a group charge of €6.50 per person. The day was dry and cloudy.

Our first venue, beside the coffee-shop, was the Historic Science Centre, which gives much attention to the famous telescope. It also treats the pioneer photography of Mary Countess of Rosse in the 1840s, and the Steam Turbine invented by her son Charles and used later in ships. We next walked through the extensive grounds, trying to absorb some of the rich variety of very old trees and exotic plants. These are labelled to give descriptions, and include 'The Carroll Oak' which is at least 500 years old. The rivers Camcor and Little Brosna meet within the demesne and provide a wildlife sanctuary, before flowing west into the Shannon. The Castle itself is still private, as the family home of the Parsons, living there since 1620 in the castle they built on the site of a Norman castle dating from 1170. The Parsons family formal title is 'Earl and Countess of Rosse.'

The inventor of the great telescope was the Third Earl of Rosse, William Parsons, born in Yorkshire on 17th June 1800 and departed this life on 31st October 1867. He was educated at Trinity College Dublin and at Magdalen College Oxford, where he graduated in Mathematics with First Class Honours in 1822. He married an English woman, Mary Field, in 1836 and they had four sons. He served as MP for King's County (now named County Offaly) in the British House of Commons during 1821-1834, starting while still at Oxford, and became an Irish Peer in the House of Lords from 1845 onwards. Recognition of his research work won him many honours, including the Order of St. Patrick. Unlike many other scientists of his time, he published full technical details of his telescopes and stellar discoveries in the best scientific journals available.

William the Earl in fact designed and built two telescopes of the 'Reflecting' kind, one having a mirror of 36 inches diameter, and the second, named 'Leviathan', having a mirror of 72-inch diameter, and being the world's largest from its first use in 1847 up to roughly 1917, a span of some seventy years. A 'reflecting' telescope lets the light from a distant object come down inside an empty cylindrical tube to reach a curved (parabolic) mirror at the bottom, which reflects and focuses it to form an image back up inside the tube. This image is caught precisely by a small slanting mirror which reflects it out through a hole in the side of the tube, so as to reach the 'Eyepiece' lens which magnifies the image as required. Sir Isaac Newton (1642-1727) also designed and used a telescope of this kind.

A restored version of Leviathan stands where it was, in the grounds. It comprised a hollow tube (of wood and metal) some 54 feet long weighing 16 tons and having at its lower end a parabolic metal mirror of diameter 72 inches. The central viewing direction was due south. It could be raised from horizontal to vertical, but with only some 10 degrees rotation to left or right possible, because of the two big sidewalls of cut stone which carried the heavy tube in a steel frame attached to the walls by ropes and geared pulley-wheels with attached counter-weights. The mirror was made of 'Speculum' metal, a mix of two-thirds copper and one-third tin, giving a highly polished surface, but reflecting only two-thirds of the light received, by comparison with more modern mirrors of glass and mercury which reflect some 90 percent of light received. With the help of only two men, the Earl was able to manipulate the 16-ton telescope so as to counteract (to some extent) the effect of Earth's rotation, which in a few seconds can move the point of interest out of the telescope's field of view if no continuous tracking adjustment is made. Nowadays an electric motor attachment can keep track of the point being viewed.

No photography was available at that time to make pictures of images in telescopes, so the Earl had to make sketches by hand of what he saw. Among many, the Owl Nebula and the Whirlpool Galaxy are notable. He discovered 226 new items as now listed in the 'New General Catalogue' (NGC) series, and gave much improved views of some 70 objects already known. The power of Leviathan is illustrated by a remark of an Irish MP colleague, Thomas Langlois Lefroy: 'Planet Jupiter is seen twice as large as the Moon appears to the naked eye.'

Only some of the data given above emerged from looking at the structure in the castle grounds. However, this writer hopes to be excused for concentrating on a world-famous telescope of its day, designed, built and used successfully by the brilliant Third Earl of Rosse, and published in detail so that others could know and use his discoveries.

Eamon Henry

Older & Bolder

Kevin's family

Older and bolder? Yes. Hopefully wiser too.

A little child looks me in the eye and says 'Grandad, will you play a game with me?' They say: 'I'll run and you catch me'. That can be difficult when the legs are not as limber as they used to be. Or they might say to me: 'Hide and they will find me.' Not so difficult.

Another grandchild will ask: 'Any jobs for me?' And you let them help with a simple task. How they love to help and their little faces light up when you praise them and say what a wonderful help they were. Another job I am asked quite often: 'Will you bring me to the shop?' How could I refuse? They keep my wife and I very busy, but it is a labour of love.

I am lucky to be a member of AITS in the Terenure Enterprise Centre. It is a great meeting place for retired people to share their experiences and learn new skills.

To the people working there you are doing a great job. Well done.

Kevin McGrath

Old Pilots

Mike and Kim

There is an old saying in aviation that there are old pilots and there are bold pilots but there are no old bold pilots. I retired from flying some years ago. The Company was offering early retirement and a golden handshake, so I took the money and ran. My poor old body was getting burnt out, and I was constantly tired from jet lag as I was on the Atlantic routes. On reflection, it was the best, or maybe the only good decision, I ever made.

I had always wanted to try my hand at writing, so I joined a creative writing group in Ballyroan library and this gave me the encouragement and stimulus I needed. I find it very interesting and am amazed at the variety and diversity the group produce. I started a degree course at The Open University and was able to complete this. I also play bridge in the Templeogue Bridge Club 2/3 nights a week. I joined a gym to keep fit and I attend Tai Chi classes. I now sometimes wonder how I ever found time to work!

Shortly after retiring I got involved with a company in San

Francisco, producing a programme in Aviation English. Among the many places I had to travel to, was Kazikstan. It is a vast country in Central Asia covering three time zones but a population of only 16 million. It was originally part on the USSR and has vast reserves of oil, gas and other minerals. Paulo Coelho has said that most of us spend 30 or 40 years working in a job we may hate, looking forward to the day of retirement; then when we do finally retire, we die a few years later from sheer boredom.

Mike Mahon

My Brother When I Was Young

Noel was my younger brother by four years, but we were close. This was mainly because of our interest in nature, wildlife and fishing.

Our family grew up in the outer Liberties of Dublin. Our father, Thomas Patrick Conneff had been born in Pimlico and our mother, Margaret Kavanagh, came from Bride Street. But Thomas Patrick could have been a country man trapped in the city. He knew more about wildlife than many a farmer I met in later life and he gifted us a marvellous and rewarding interest in nature.

Noel contracted Diphtheria when he was three years old and was taken from us and sent to Clonskeagh Fever Hospital. We children were not allowed to visit him. My father would travel on his bicycle and would get to see him through a small viewing panel. But Noel could not see his Dad. That, it was decided by the Hospital people, would have unsettled Noel and made him want to come home. If I remember correctly, my mother never got to see her little son in hospital. She had to rely on my father's reports for news of his recovery and she was forced to wait for a full four and a half months before she got him back.

If this trauma was to affect Noel in later life, it seems only to have made him gentler. He grew up with a great love of animals and birds in trouble. Many a broken wing was repaired or a small animal nursed back to health in our back garden in Hamilton Street. Most memorable among our patients there was 'Herbie', the young seagull. He arrived with a broken wing. I do not remember where exactly Noel found him, but I do know that we fed and nursed that bird for months on end, for almost a year in fact. It became a great pet and a part of the family. Then one day, Herbie was gone. We worried that a cat had taken him but we should have known. The seagull had a fearsome beak. He would have been able to defend himself. In the event, Herbie was found later that day, hale and hearty. He was taking a stroll in the general neighbourhood of Donore Road. Clearly his ability to fly was coming back and we were soon going to lose him and this did happen. Gradually the escape flights grew longer. Then one day, we could not find him and had to accept that he was by now fully on the wing.

On most Sunday mornings the whole family, with the exception of my mother and sister, would go for a walk along the Grand Canal. We would commence at Sally's Bridge and generally move towards Dolphin's barn. Our father would point out to us the varied wildlife along this city waterway. Mallard ducks, swans, water hens, coots and water rats were all to be seen in their natural environment. There was also the odd Muscovy migrant duck from St. Stephen's green and of course we saw the fish. There were perch, rudd, eels, stickleback, gudgeon and the lordly bream. I remember my father being particularly impressed by the black bars on the yellow and vermillion coloured fins of the perch, which he usually referred to as the 'dandy of the fresh water.'

When the inevitable canal boat came along, the water became muddied and we lost sight of our finny friends. Then to the accompaniment of the sound of the bells of Christ Church and St. Patrick's Cathedrals, we would wend our way home to our dinner at 1.30 PM.

Over the years, Noel and I continued with our hobbies in the back garden. When he diverted into homing pigeons, I decided to create a small pond. While my brother built a loft with timber and wire mesh, I retrieved an old enamelled baby bath which had served the family well in its day. The bath had several small holes in it, which I repaired with traditional pot menders. After sinking the bath in the ground, I planted some water lilies in it and very soon it was populated with 103 pinkeens (sticklebacks and minnows), mostly caught in the Dodder river at Rathfarnham. As I graduated to angling, I managed to catch a few red-finned rudd and perch in the canal, which lodged with us for a while before being returned to their original home under Sally's Bridge.

Noel for his part did have some success with his homing pigeons and actually managed to win a few races with them and true to form, he nursed an orphan bird whose mother did not return home after a race, by hand feeding it with Indian corn soaked in warm milk. It grew up to be a pet for us all and was much loved. It was a slate-blue colour with white wings. We called it 'Pip'. Although Noel did not send Pip to race, the pesky bird still managed to get lost once. He survived to return miraculously however after three or four days. It turned out that, while perched on the roof, he had slipped and fallen down our next door neighbour's chimney.

Ms Healy had been having trouble lighting her fire. 'There is some sort of blockage in the flue,' she was saying, 'and scratching noises as well. Something is up there'. Eventually, a totally black soot covered bird emerged into the hearth. It was an emaciated Pip the pet pigeon. How he had survived, without food or water for the duration was hard to understand. But Noel cleaned him up, hand fed him for the second time in his life and nursed him back to health.

Noel and I continued our interests together, particularly angling into later life. This was despite the fact that he met and married a Scots girl called Myra Duncan and went to live in Mount Florida, Glasgow. Through this, I got to fish for trout in the River Clyde, which was being cleaned up then after the waning of heavy industry, and also in the world famous Lough Leven. I also visited the great Falls of Clyde and many of the other sights of Alba.

Noel died in Scotland three years ago. I miss him sorely.

Ar dheis Dé go raibh a anam Dílis.

Paddy Conneff

Time To Reflect

Phena on Concern duties

I have stopped rushing about, stopped 'getting there' and sometimes take time to prepare for that fourth part of my life, called Eternity. I don't worry much and have discovered that life is not quite as serious as I made it out to be. I am lucky to have time left to reflect a little.

I got the opportunity of taking early retirement from my great career, and when asked by well meaning people what will you do now, I said I would love to do two things - keep chickens and learn to play the banjo!

Well I haven't had time to do either. Oh, the joy of a leisurely breakfast, a walk in the sunshine or rain. I have watched my robin take crumbs from my hand and have had time to talk to my friends.

On the action side, I have joined a book club, played golf, walked the prom and swam in Galway Bay with pure delight. I have been involved with Concern since 1982 and since retiring, have worked with them in Somalia, Rwanda, Sudan and Afghanistan. It's been an honour and I'm so lucky to be still useful! My role was mainly sourcing and setting up housing for the many volunteers who work with the poorest people in the developing world and to give them some comforts and rest. Being with the poorest has taught me never to complain again. They have so little, accept so much and have taught me a lot. I discovered from a great lady in Bangladesh that one can live, owning a mat, two saris and a bowl and still smile! What a discovery for me as I get older and bolder.

And I still might get time to keep chickens and play that banjo!

Phena O' Boyle

Teabags

My first encounter with a tea bag was in the mid fifties. My brother and I were travelling from Shannon to Toronto via New York and we arrived at the International Airport very early in the morning. Not as yet having had breakfast and feeling hungry, we proceeded to the café to get something to eat. We ordered Bacon, Egg, Sausage, the usual trimmings and tea, all of which arrived very promptly, except the tea, that is. You see the custom in those days was that the waitress arrived at your table with glasses of water as she brought the menu first thing. Well, the meal came and we tucked into it with gusto, and then called for the tea. What a surprise, a pot of lukewarm water and two cups each with a whiteish looking bag thing in it, and a string hanging over the side of the cup with a small label at the end - no milk or sugar but a slice of lemon. This was the first time we really knew what the expression meant – 'dishwater.' Fast forward several years. I had settled down to living and working in Toronto, having brought my wife and young family out to share in the good life. We made many friends, amongst them a couple from a small village in rural Ireland. It was customary for this couple to send a parcel home to Ireland every so often, and in one of these they included a packet of tea bags for the folks at home to try. Again it was the custom to arrange a phone call, no small undertaking in those days, especially, say, at Christmas time. Well, the phone call having taken place and all the usual gossip and news exchanged, it was time to enquire about the most recent parcel and, by the way, how did they like the tea? 'Oh, it was very good,' came the reply; then a slight pause, 'but it was an awful nuisance having to cut open each individual packet.'

Albert Connor

It's A Dogs Life

At a recent night at the dogs in Harold's Cross I was reminded of years ago when my family reared greyhounds, and the night we had entered our best one at the Galway track. My brother, his brother-in-law and myself, prepared to bring the dog - called 'The Two Franks' after themselves - by putting me and the dog into the back of the vehicle, or as they say in the West, 'the ould vaneen', while they rode in state in the front. We arrived in Galway in good time and after some preliminaries, our dog was entered to run in the third race. We adjourned to the stand leaving the dog in good care with the handlers and waited with growing excitement for the third race. Sure enough, out onto the track came 'The Two Franks', looking good – so well he might, after my brother spending every spare hour he had weeks before feeding him brown bread and exercising him twice a day, all to my parents amusement!

Out of the traps and away with them around the track. And sure enough 'The Two Franks' came storming in first. Great excitement! I was detailed to take charge of the dog after the lead was put on him, and to stay right there until they came back from the Secretary's office, where they were going to collect their prize.

After a long delay, I saw the two men coming towards me, staggering with laughter. Oh, I thought they must have got huge prize money, but as they came nearer I noticed the mood had changed. 'You got a great prize,' I said. 'No. No,' they said, 'we didn't win.' 'We didn't win?' I asked incredulously. 'Of course we won – what are you talking about?' 'No, we didn't – we were disqualified.' 'Disqualified,' I asked, 'For what?' 'For biting. We should have had 'The Two Franks' muzzled because of his biting - so he was disqualified.' 'O dear. Whatever will Mam say? She will be so disappointed.'

Anyway, all the way home we either laughed or cried – between the men imitating the Secretary stammering out his reason for disqualification – looking for all the world like a character out of Dickens - and the loss of the big prize!!

Maureen Maloney

When I Retired

When I retired from the Civil Service I thought my life was going to be very boring. So I set about getting busy to fill in the working hours. I was a member of Newland's Golf Club and loved the sport. My friends played there and we had a good social life. In 1996 I got my Swimming Teacher's Exam and received my certificate from The Lord Mayor. I taught in Terenure College swimming pool. I enjoyed teaching the nervous adults and I especially loved teaching children. I taught for twenty years and decided to give it up when all my grand children could swim. I am still playing golf and love it. When I was younger I played on golf teams, and in 1982 was Lady Captain. I now help with the Junior Section and taught my grandchildren to play.

I joined so many things that I filled every minute of the day. This went on for years until I had a terrible car accident with my granddaughter. We were turning in to Terenure College when a speeding car crashed into ours and turned us over. We both crawled out with just a scratch. It must have been heavenly intervention and the Good Lord was not ready for me yet. From that day on I said my prayers more fervently.

Last Christmas, Santa sent me a lap top and what a joy I am getting from it. It's like a new toy. Last year, I joined the Active Senior IT Society in the Terenure Enterprise Centre. This year I joined the classes in Creative Writing. Our tutor is Rick Quinn. He gives us lots of encouragement. I am fascinated listening to all the people of my own age recounting their experiences of life and work.

Eileen Williamson

My Son was Accident Prone

T om was accident prone from very early on. There was not very much of him that hadn't been seen or treated in Crumlin Hospital. Truth to tell I had got to the stage of letting him relate his own problems, so fearful had I become that he might be considered a battered child. He fell off walls, crashed bicycles and famously caught his head in the gate. He managed to run into a stationary car and almost remove his nose on the fender.

One thing was constant with him, once mother appeared and he was mopped up and cleaned up to ascertain the damage, he calmed down. With my hand firmly clasped in his, he resigned himself to the inevitable. One particularly large gash necessitated so many stitches that I lost count. We returned to the hospital a week later to have them removed but looking at the wound I realised they had healed a bit too tightly and it was going to be traumatic for him.

'What will they do?' he asked. I explained they would snip the stitches very quickly with a scissors very similar to the one we had in the kitchen drawer. If he was very brave he could probably bring one or two home to show Dan and Barry and Al. This cheered him up no end and we reached the steps of the hospital.

By this time I wasn't feeling quite so brave and I realised my hands had begun to shake. Fearful that I would transfer my fear to him, I let go of his hand on the pretext of pointing out the doorway and he went in without a worry in the world. Exactly as I had predicted the nurse had a tray with an array of scissors, and he let her get on with the job. In no time at all - to my great relief - we were back out on the steps of the hospital with his hand very firmly clasped in mine once more.

Fia Weber

My Sporting Life

Clanna Gael GAA Club

N o words of mine can do justice to the wonderful joy, excitement, passion and life-long friends I made while playing sport and being involved. From a very young age I tried my hand at running, high jump, long jump, hop skip and jump but Gaelic football and handball won out.

As a youth I joined our local GAA club, St Brendan's, Killina, County Roscommon. We practised and played against other neighboring teams. The competition and struggle to win was intense. If we won it was wonderful, but if we lost, we went down home downhearted. But not for long. We practised and played our next game with more determination.

At that time we didn't have the luxury of dressing rooms and showers. We togged out under the trees in the sports field and would leave our clothes out in the open while we played the game. It was normal practice then. Sports gear was also a luxury at that time. Sometimes I borrowed football boots and gear from a friend. Jerseys were the only items that were supplied by the club.

I played handball at that time also. The nearest ball alley was by the lakeside at Drynan Lake. At that time handballs were very scarce. Often during a game if a ball went out over the top of the alley, it could take one or two hours searching before it was found and the game continued. They were wonderful care-free times that I look back on now with great fondness.

In 1955, at 19 years of age, I came to work in Dublin where I joined Benburb's club. It was great help to me settling in and making new friends. I also kept in touch with St Brendan's, the home club, where my friend John would write pleading with me to come home as there was a very important game to play. I did not need much persuasion to oblige. At times my girlfriend was not too happy with me deserting her for the GAA. That all worked out in the end.

I joined Clanna Gael, one of the bigger clubs in Dublin at that time. After practice on a Wednesday evening in St Anne's Park, we would all go to the Teachers' Club in Parnell Square, where the club held a dance. These were very enjoyable times.

Around that time I also became a steward at Croke Park, which lasted for about 40 years. It was a great honour to be there for all the big sporting occasions. My only regret was I was not a steward when the GAA allowed soccer and rugby to be played.

I will conclude now by saying I had a very happy and enjoyable life and sport played a very important part in it.

Kevin Mc Grath

My Life Today

Pauline's family

At last, I am free to decide how I will spend the long-awaited bonus of free time which comes with retirement. My husband had retired earlier, and patiently waited for the day when we could both take off on some of our long-planned travels. We started on a high by sailing from Southampton to America on the Queen Mary. Six days of luxury on board was followed by three weeks of touring the United States on the Amtrak train network. More recent trips have included studying Spanish in Madrid, teaching English to Spanish people in Barcelona and visiting Morocco. A return visit to Sardinia is our next destination.

In between our travels, we enjoy quality time with our twelve grandchildren, although not usually altogether! We find time with the younger generation works better for everyone when the parents are absent as, having a family of six, which has now virtually doubled with the addition of their wonderful partners, it can sometimes be difficult to get a word in, so our family get-togethers need lots of planning but are always very rewarding and enjoyable.

Volunteering plays a small part in my life nowadays. I assist in a local charity shop and serve as a board member of the Terenure Enterprise Centre.

My wish now is for continued good health to appreciate my good fortune.

Pauline Doyle

A Cottage In The Country

My sister rang from Wexford. 'I've just been out to see that cottage you mentioned,' she said, 'and to my surprise it has four walls and a roof. I think you had better come and have a look for yourself.' We collected the keys one bright spring Saturday morning, and set out to view the property. Dank, dirty and abandoned as it was, it stood on high ground on nearly an acre. From the front door the beautiful countryside spread out on all sides as far as the eye could see. It was completely irresistible. Husband Paul was equally enthusiastic. Instead of changing my decrepit banger for an updated model, we bought a cottage in Glenbrien. Children, family and friends thought we were stone mad!!

It took a long, long time to make it habitable, but did we have fun! We were like two kids again with a dolls house, planning and arguing over every move. Some things we didn't change. Old window shutters were carefully refurbished. The wide fireplace stayed, albeit with a stove installed. A craftsman in the town replicated the old doors that were missing or beyond repair, complete with latches. All the original beams were scrubbed. The charred ones at the window, where the Tailor Gray (a previous inhabitant) had sat cross-legged on a high table with an oil lamp to light his fine stitching, didn't respond. They remained exactly the same as they had been since the early part of the last century.

The gardens came to life after backbreaking work, and the neighbours came to call. 'You know of course that Mr. Gray won best in Leinster with this garden,' they said. It seemed they had forgotten the intervening thirty something years which produced a forest of weeds that had grown higher than the house itself. Our builder filled a marl hole in the village with the debris and we created our beautiful cottage garden from scratch.

We had a many years of total pleasure there in our idyllic place in the country. I think the Tailor Gray would have been pleased with what we did with his house. We certainly were, and family and friends came and stayed and loved it almost as much as we did, for many years afterwards.

Fia Weber

Trams

Old Dublin Tram

I knew about travelling on buses, but a tram! Well a tram was a different mode of transport altogether. The tram I was to travel on was in O'Connell Street in Dublin and I was about four years old. It was probably in the early 1940's.

The tram did not pull alongside the kerb like the bus did. Instead I had to step off the footpath and make my way across to a central island where the tram was waiting. The street was busy with horse drawn traffic and bicycles, and buses, and I had to be careful.

The tram or tramcar as it was called had metal wheels which sat on grooved metal tracks and these were set in cobblestones which were very bumpy to walk on. Above the tram ran electric cables and an arm reached up from the tram to connect with the cable. This arm was called a trolley pole and it always faced backwards and it was through this that the tram was powered.

This tram had an upstairs like a double-decker bus reached by a semi spiral staircase but unlike the buses I travelled in, the upper deck was completely open to the skies. The backs of the seats were interesting. They moved backwards and forwards on a central pivot and why was this? Well, it is because trams cannot turn around. They can only go back and forth so they had a driving section with a set of control levers and a staircase at each end.

The B.K.T. or Blackrock Kingstown electric tramline from Nelson Pillar, Dublin to Marine Road, Kingstown closed on 9th July 1949. Today Kingstown is known as Dun Laoghaire.

Opal Peard

Chieftain

Kevin Conneff

U nlike my colleagues in the Chieftains, I did not grow up in a traditional music home, but the wireless was to prove an important part of my formative years. Although I was mostly interested in the pop music of the day (Guy Mitchell, Patti Page or the early rock 'n rollers, Elvis, Brenda Lee et al), I do remember the whole family listening to Céilí House, Clais Céadaí an Radió and my sister, Áine, getting up from the table to dance to whatever céilí band was on The Mitchelstown Creameries sponsored programme.

Tenors were my father's favourite; so if McCormack, Gigli or Caruso were being played, we'd all have to be absolutely silent until the scratchy recording finished and my father's eyes would open again. Ciarán MacMathúna's Ceólta Tíre would also be listened to, but only got my father's attention if a flute or whistle was being played. Fiddles or uileann pipes were usually not to his liking. 'Off key,' he would say. Years later, one of my band colleagues, when I told him this, said, 'he was probably right some of the time!'

There was one exception to the father's distain for fiddlers; the great Sean Maguire. And Sean's playing brought as many shivers to my own spine as did the singing of Elvis or Little Richard.

When growing up in the outer Liberties of Donore, I was unaware of the work of the people behind the street names. Petrie Road and O Carolan Road were named in honour of the great collector and great composer respectively. And, when going to work in the mornings, I'd often have the pleasure of being accompanied by Mr. Welsh, a partially blind gentleman from a house across from ours in Hamilton Street, down Ebenezer Terrace and through Cow Parlour to Weaver's Square. Mr. Welsh (Pádraig Breathnach) and his nephew Declan Welsh were literally the last of the weavers. Pádraig's son, Breandán, would record traditional music and publish 'Ceól', a quarterly journal of Irish music, which he insisted should never cost more than the price of a pint! He also compiled and published 'Ceól Rinnce na hÉireann', which along with O'Neill's collection is an essential possession of any aspiring traditional musician. Also, although I did not know him then, a founder member of the Chieftains, Sean Potts, lived and grew up not far away, at No. 6 The Coombe and has written a beautiful air in honour of his home.

I announced at age 15 that I had a job as a photographic assistant. This entailed sweeping floors and putting down rat poison in a basement in Clare Street, while the man I was supposed to be learning from, was reluctant to teach me anything lest he weaken his own position there. Some of the lads with whom I worked (they were mechanics for office machinery) were very interested in Irish music, which is how a sixteen year old Elvis look alike (I thought!) went to his first fleadhanna ceoil in Mullingar and Elphin. It was there that I first encountered traditional musicians playing live and I was completely smitten.

In the sixties and seventies I became involved with the run-

ning of the Tradition Club in Slattery's of Capel Street. The Tra-
dition Club's aim was to give a stage to pure traditional musi-
cians and singers at a time when the ballad and folk boom had
many venues in Dublin. In June 1976 I got a phone call from
Paddy Moloney at my place of work (a printing firm in Lr. Bag-
got Street) asking me if I could go to London in early July to put
bodhran on a couple of tracks of an album the Chieftains were
recording. Halfway through that week's recording session,
Paddy asked me to join the band and after a couple of weeks
pondering I decided to join the Chieftains, but was adamant I'd
go back to a nine to five job after a couple of years. That was 35
years ago and I'm still touring the world as a Chieftain.

When I stand for my solo song in the Chieftains programme
on the stage at Carnegie Hall I think to myself 'The Greats, Gigli
and Caruso and Callas stood here; Count Basie, Benny Good-
man stood here – what the **** am I doing here!?' But then I
think, I'm in a band with Paddy Moloney, Sean Keane and Matt
Molloy and they are definite 'greats' of Irish Music.

Maybe I'll sing the *'Pride of Pimlico.'*

Kevin Conneff

How I became involved with the computer

W hen I was in my early sixties I realised that quite a lot of people I knew were into computers and I felt I was being left behind, so I decided to do something about it. So, I enrolled at my local Fás course for a starter course in computers. At that time I did not know how to switch one on. I knew absolutely nothing about computers. A lot of people including myself were afraid of computers being complicated, which they are not. I started the course, shall we say at the beginning switch on the computer, learn how to click a mouse, how to write a sentence and do alterations i.e. if you miss a word how do you slot it in. Also how to cut and paste. The course consisted of Word and Excel. Word is writing a text like I am doing now. Excel is different. It consists of a lot of horizontal lines and some vertical lines. It is used for doing accounts and other things, as well to do with figures. I now do all my accounts on Excel. We were also taught how to save on a floppy disc, which of course we don't use any longer. We now save on a memory stick.

Having got all that knowledge, I decided to go a stage further and do my ECDL. This involved seven modules. The modules I was most interested in were emails and Internet. I help my wife find words for her crossword on Google and I find Google Earth very interesting. Also, I even find myself playing Jedward for my grandchildren on You Tube.

I wouldn't be without my computer now. I use it everyday. If you want to learn about computers the best place to start is at the beginning.

Sean Gallagher

Happy Surfing

S o, your kids or grandkids have been forced to move to Australia. You write regularly and phone when you can but they are on the other side of the world and it just doesn't feel the same. So what do you do? Well, if you have email and instant messaging you can have conversations in real time and if you use a computer device called 'Skype', which is a web camera, then you can actually look at them on your computer screen and talk as if both of you were on television. This is just one of the many cheap and incredibly easy benefits of knowing how to use your computer to the best of its ability.

To the untrained eye, all matters computer can seem very daunting and off putting. But relax, it's as easy as pie. Can't find that book you've been looking for in any bookshop? Then just log on to amazon.com, the website that is, effectively, the biggest bookshop in the world, where all you have to do is type in the name of the book/record/movie you want and in two or three days it will arrive at your doorstep. You need to get some groceries but the weather is atrocious and, anyway, you have people coming around and you don't want to miss them? Just email Tesco or Superquinn with your order and they will have it delivered to your door within the hour.

This is the joy of the internet and it's something that people who don't use it often don't understand – the internet works for you, not the other way around.

Starting anything you have never done before is always going to be a difficult task. After all, when you are stepping into the unknown there will always be a degree of worry. But once you get used to logging on to your favourite websites and using the internet to talk to friends and loved ones there will be no stopping you. Because the internet is the greatest communications tool we have ever had. You can talk to people all over the world for free and despite the image some people have of internet users as being strange young Americans who talk in an incomprehensible language and might as well be rocket scientists for all their jargon, going online is incredibly simple, quick and easy.

But most importantly of, going online is fun. That tends not to be mentioned very often but you can spend hours just surfing the net exploring new areas and opening new horizons with each click of a button.

So remember this – embrace it, enjoy it, and don't ever, ever be worried about getting the hang of it because you will have the whole thing worked out shortly after you try it for the first time.

Ian O'Doherty

Finding The Good In Others

John Lonergan

During my time as Governor of Mountjoy Prison (1984/2010) we had a wonderful project called 'The Mountjoy Prison Community Works Project.' First established in 1978, it operated for over 30 years, directly providing excellent facilities for many communities throughout Dublin city and county. The works party was made up of six to eight male prisoners, who were released every day from the prison to work in the community under the direction and supervision of two outstanding prison officers, Niall McGrory and Paddy Moloney. Over the 30 years of its existence, the works party built or refurbished over twenty community centres and other vital facilities for many small local communities, who could not afford to hire outside contactors to undertake the work.

In 2002, the works party was invited by Father Dermot Leycock, Parish Priest at St. Brigid's in Killester, to build a family and community resource centre in the grounds attached to the local church. During the building of the centre, the parish acquired some extra land, and it was decided to use it to provide extra car parking facilities at the church. The final stage was to build a new high brick wall around the car park to secure it.

As luck would have it, at that time two young men from the Midlands area, who were qualified brick layers, were serving prison sentences in Mountjoy. They were immediately assigned to the works project and began working on erecting the wall. Everything went brilliantly and the wall was soon taking shape. Then word came through from the Irish Prison Service that the two men were granted temporary release and allowed to go home. They were delighted with their good fortune, and when they told Father Dermot their good news, he wished them the very best and then it struck him: 'but what about the wall, what will we do now?' 'Don't worry Father we'll be back.' With broad smiles on their faces, off they went.

Early the following Saturday morning, Fr. Dermot saw a small truck drive into the church grounds, and out jumped the two boys. 'We're back to finish the wall, Father.'

The centre was officially open by President Mary McAleese in September 2004.

John Lonergan

St Brigid's Resource Centre

Writing

Mary Butler

I am now putting one of the golden rules for writing into prac-
tice by 'applying the seat of my pants to the seat of my chair'
with pen in hand and a blank sheet of paper in front of me and
see what happens.

My thoughts ramble back to my early schooldays and the
procedure leading up to the writing period each day. We had to
put all our books away and the good blue and red lined copies,
which were kept in a press in the classroom, were distributed.
The little round inkwells in the desks were filled with black ink
from a big bottle. Then with a square of blotting paper placed
under my right hand. I would dip the wooden handle pen with
the silver/golden nib into the ink and copy the letters written on
the blackboard. We progressed from words to sentences and by
the time we had progressed to the single line copies we were writ-
ing short stories. I enjoyed writing these in primary school. It
was a different kettle of fish when I was in secondary school. I
remember ruling as wide a margin as I could possibly get away
with and stretching each letter in order to fill the pages when I
found it difficult to write on certain topics.

I remember when I was in fourth year and I wrote an essay,

which suggested a different type of approach to a certain subject. Well, the teacher called me up to her desk and in a very cross voice asked me what type of rubbish was this. She put her pen through it and wouldn't entertain such ideas. I went back to my desk feeling very hurt and rejected and I felt I wouldn't try any-thing like that again - so much for encouraging creative writing!

I left Ballina when I was 19 and got a job in Dublin. We didn't have a phone at home so every week I would write a newsy letter home and my mother would write back to me. I looked forward to my weekly letter. My mother had beautiful handwrit-ing and I would feel her warmth as I read the letters.

Years later when my mother started to phone me I missed the letters. I think there is something special about getting a letter. Every Christmas there are a few special friends that I still write to. It's a bit more effort but the advantage is of being able to sit down and take time to think of the news. I would then hope that my effort would be reciprocated and look forward to finding a few lines enclosed in the Christmas cards from those friends. I find writing very therapeutic. I find it's a great way of express-ing any emotion that is causing me stress and anxiety. I can write about anything I feel and nobody has to see it. It releases that emotion thereby freeing me of the resulting stress thus help-ing me to deal with the situation in a more rational manner. I then have the choice to keep it and have it as a reminder of what I had felt at that particular time or tear it up and be finished with it. To reinforce the golden rule I referred to in my first paragraph I was browsing through a book on the business of writing and it said - one of the best pieces of advice given to any writer is an old axiom 'Don't get it right – get it written.'

Mary Butler

Angels

My first introduction to Angels was the prayer 'O Angel of God my Guardian dear....' The image I had was of two angelic spirits clad in white robes with big wings to protect me. I would say the prayer every morning and evening never thinking much about the meaning of the words.

I had a younger sister Ann who died when she was two years and six months old. I remember the little white coffin being carried from our house and my father placing it on his lap in the backseat of Jim Corcoran's hackney car. She was taken to League cemetery where she was buried with my father's mother and his two sisters who also died when they were very young. We were told that Ann had gone to Heaven and was now a little Angel.

In the practice of Reiki, the Ark Angels are called upon for Protection and Healing. They are depicted by their colour and virtues e.g. Gabriel's colour is White Crystal and his virtues are: Purity, Resurrection, Artistic Development and Concentration. He was sent to tell Mary that she was to become the mother of God so I understood from a young age that Angels were God's messengers. I always enjoyed singing the Christmas carol 'Angels we have heard on high, sweetly singing o'er the plains.' Angels seem to be happy troopers - singing, free flowing spirits bringing good news. Sounds like a nice job to me. I wonder what the qualifications are! Do they take on new recruits? The Gárda Relief Force comes to my mind. How would one apply? Would I be considered for such a job? These are some of the questions I ask myself as I think about the Angels.

Mary Butler

Short Stories

Bob's Christmas

Rick Quinn

E very year in the days running up to Christmas it had been
Bob's routine to work all the hours he could, entertaining
some of his bigger clients and delivering bottles of whiskey to
others who expected them.

Needless to say, this didn't go down too well with his wife,
Marie. 'Your own wife and family come last as usual.'

This year to forestall any trouble, Bob negotiated with Marie:
'I'll pick you and the kids up outside the Central Hotel at 2
o'clock on the dot. We'll all go to lunch and then it's off to visit
Santa Claus. OK? '

He pulled on his nose. This was always a dead giveaway that
he wasn't sure how well his words were being received.
And this time, Marie laid down the law: 'Be there … on time or
else … and no excuses.'

His duties out of the way, Bob left the office in plenty of
time. He crossed the road to where he had parked his car earlier,
a few yards away from the gates of Donore Avenue Church.

'O my God! The effing hearse. Who parked the effing hearse
there?' A large black Mercedes was blocking his car and there
was no way he could get out.

Bob paced up and down. He felt his blood pressure mounting. He lit a cigarette. It dropped out of his shaking hand. Tension was building up to high doh. Visions of Marie's face flashed before him.

He forced himself to think straight. He looked around. No men in black suits in sight. He weighed up one scenario. To march into the church. Up to the driver of the hearse. In front of everyone demand: 'Are you the driver of that hearse. Would you mind moving it right away?' He baulked at this.

Then something made him look inside the hearse. There dangling from the ignition was a bunch of keys. He took a deep breath. He sneaked a quick look over his shoulder towards the church door. He sat into the plush leather seat of the hearse and turned the key in the ignition. A sigh from Bob when the engine purred quietly. The gearbox was automatic and it took what seemed to take for ever to find reverse gear. He backed the hearse up a few yards.

He leapt into his own car. It was 2 o'clock. He sped down the quays in the direction of the Central Hotel. Every traffic light was red. At the last red light his arm jerked against his jacket pocket. A metallic jingle. He was gripped with horror. 'O God, it's the keys of the hearse!'

In a cold sweat, Bob swung the car, tyres squealing, over the next bridge and scorched back in the direction of the church. A bemused crowd of mourners was huddled around the hearse. They were trying not to look at the coffin resting inside it. The driver stood dumbstruck scratching his head under his peaked cap. Bob leapt out of his car. He stuffed the keys of the hearse into the driver's hand. Before the driver could recover his speech, Bob was gone.

Bob survived another nightmare drive back to the Central Hotel. There they were. Marie standing stock still, holding the

hands of her children.   A frozen tableau transfixed against the lights of the quay.
All the lights were against me,' was all Bob could manage.

He pulled on his nose.

Rick Quinn

Shamie's Birthday

Mike Mahon

Today is Shamie's birthday. A special day for most kids, but Shamie didn't feel any different, any bigger, any older, any wiser. He sat, as he did most days on O'Connell Bridge, a cardboard box at his feet, hoping for a few cents from indifferent passer-by's. It was November; 'the hardiest childer are born in winter,' his Ma had often said before he had seen her laid in the cold grave, leaving him in the tender care of his father, a hard man. He shivered and picked at the scabs on his bare knees, marks from the last beating he'd received.

Still today was his birthday and Da had promised him a double burger and chips if he did well. He wiped a drip from his nose, pulled a harmonica from his pocket and played a few bars of Dicey Reilly. A grey wind blew up from the river. A few flecks of sleet settled on his freckled face. 'Spare a copper mam, for a cuppa tay.' Purposeful eyes avoided his pathetic gaze. 'Ya mane oul bitch.' The money was beginning to build up now. 'Should nearly be enough to keep Da happy,' he thought. 'Buy him another few more hours drinking. Keep him off my back, anyways.' Shamie needed a piss. He tried to stand but his legs were too numb with the cold and folded under him. He couldn't hold it any longer. The warm urine flooded his trousers and warmed his thighs. Most passed with eyes averted; some swung out towards the pavement; some mumbled, 'no change'; a few tossed some coins at him. None looked him in the eye. 'Am I fecking invisible or wha', Shamie thought to himself. It was getting dark. He was feeling drowsy. A heavy fist caught him on the side of the head. His face smashed against the concrete parapet. Blood mingled with the snots on his nose. His eyes welled with tears blurred. 'Sleeping on the job were ya, ya young whelp? I'll larne ya. Is this all ya have?'

'Da, I'm sorry Da. Don't hit me again Da. It's me birthday, ya promised.' He tried to gather the few scattered coins but his fingers failed him. The heavy boot smashed into his ribs. Shamie lay still. To move now was fatal. He whimpered and tasted the salty tang of his tears. Next year, maybe next year his birthday would be better.

Mike Mahon

A Good Neighbour

The Irish Civil War of 1922-23 is the source of the following story, with names of places and persons changed. Harry Martin worked a small farm in west Galway. He was a noted Free State supporter and had canvassed for their party in various local elections prior to 1922. His local importance as a 'Freestater' made him a prime target for elimination by the hard men of the other side. It so happened that around this time, at age thirty, he sometimes came and lived alone in the farmhouse on his land, as farm work required it. This farmhouse was a simple one-storey cottage, having a kitchen and two bedrooms, with front and back doors to the kitchen.

Living in a rather different environment was John Sweeney, also aged about thirty, and a neighbour of Harry. From being a casual labourer, John had joined the 'Connaught Rangers' section of the British Army. During the 1914-18 War, first at the Dardanelles and later in the trenches of the Western Front, he had survived where so many had been killed. He was horrified and sickened by what he had experienced, and looked for only a frugal but better way of life back at home, after being de-mobbed in due course.

John returned home and then worked on a casual basis on the farms of two of the hard men of our story. In their plot to kill Harry, ex-soldier John was recruited to take a shotgun on the outing, as a back-up member of the team. In the circumstances, a refusal would at least cost him their available employment, if not having more serious consequences. John thus became a very reluctant member of the execution squad. However, he was extremely careful to conceal his inner feelings.

The plan of attack was simple. John with the shotgun was to watch the back door. The other two men would force open the front door and try to confront Harry within. This would be done after midnight to reduce the risk of possible spectators and hope-fully to catch Harry asleep in bed.

What the assassins did not know was that whenever he stayed overnight at the farm, Harry lived in a state of high alert. This involved staying fully dressed at all times, and sleeping on a settle-bed in the kitchen. He kept his kitchen back-door only slightly bolted, but the two bedroom doors he kept locked. His windows already had steel bars fitted on the inside to prevent thieves from entering, so that a window smash-and-enter was not possible. His kitchen front-door was locked and also heavily bolted. He used no lights indoors, except for the occasional lighted candle in the days before rural electric power.

The night of the attack was in late October, calm and dry but cloudy, with a small half-moon, and thus fairly dark. John was quite clear in his mind. He was not going to shoot a neighbour, a man he had known from their childhood 'national school' days together. Their fathers and grandfathers had been neighbours and friendly. In John's simple heart the feeling of 'old decency' was quite strong. He would not let any lunatic make him kill his neighbour Harry.

When they arrived very quietly on foot, John with a double-barrel shotgun was sent around the side of the house, to take a suitable stance on one side of the back-door. Their assault on the front-door, which did not yield as they had expected, imme-diately aroused Harry. He quickly and quietly passed out through the kitchen back-door and pulled it shut behind him.

John stepped towards Harry and said in a whisper 'Quiet, Harry! This is me - John. Run for it out the back, and you'll be safe enough.' John could still hear the sounds of banging con-tinuing inside the cottage. The two men, on entry through the front door in almost total darkness, found the kitchen apparently empty. Their next targets were the bedroom doors, which being locked resisted strongly their attempts to burst them open. And then, with Harry safely away and running through his own fields at the back, John fired one shot up into the air. At this sound the banging inside stopped, and the two men came out the front-door and hurried around to the back. They found John bent down, as he searched through a cabbage plot. A break in the clouds let some more moonlight come through. John spoke briefly 'I think he fell in the cabbage. In such bad light I can't be sure.' Further searching found no dead Harry among the cabbage. The search was abandoned and the men went home.

Some time later, when things had settled down, Harry returned to grow crops on his farm, although he never again lived in the farmhouse. He found a wife and there were children. It caused some surprise among those who did not know the full story, how Harry and John became such close friends in the years that followed.

Eamon Henry

See No Evil, Here No Evil, Speak No Evil

T his phrase refers to an African idol of three monkeys, each one with his hands clamped over his eyes, or his ears, or his mouth. Sound advice one might have thought, but I feel I have to query the concepts. What of 'See no Evil' when there is so much evil around us in the world, mostly man-made? Is this suggesting we should all turn a blind eye to wars, acts of terrorism, crime, child abuse, rape and famine? Should we exclude the acts of many governments and multinationals? If all these evil deeds were to be ignored why then would we need police, courts or even a legal system? Should we all pretend we are living in the TV series: 'The Little House on the Prairie' and John Boy is just coming back from his fishing trip, and all sitting down to supper as one big happy blind family? If this attitude were to be pursued we would all be living in cloud cuckoo land and hoping we would never lose our rose tinted glasses. Surely, this is a form of denial; that bankers are honest people, politicians act for the good of society, or that the wheel had not been invented.

'Hear no Evil.' Well, we all have television and radio, so all one has to do is listen to the daily news bulletin, guaranteed to be mostly bad news. Even the weather forecast is always: 'Rain spreading from the West,' and the worse it is the more we talk about it, taking perverse pleasure in our climate. Then sometimes we get a few days of sunshine and no rain. Suddenly the country is in a state of chaos, there are water shortages in the cities and the farmers are complaining of the drought! It appears God can't win. Some years ago in the USA some publisher decided to produce a newspaper that would only print good news. It was a flop; people only wanted news of disasters. Is there something terribly wrong with the human psyche? Even in our daily conversations we seem to take morbid pleasure in spreading gossip. 'Did you hear Mrs. Grogan husband has gone off with a

pole dancer?' 'Well, she's better off without him.' 'Yea, but un-
fortunately he keeps coming back.' The son asks his mother if he
were adopted. She replied, 'Yes, but they gave you back!' Funer-
als attract bigger crowds than weddings, although nobody gets in-
vited. 'What did poor old Frank die from?' 'Ah, it was nothing
too serious anyway.' And why are priests and nuns always telling
kids: 'You're going to end up in hell.'

Finally, 'Speak no Evil'. Well this appears to make some
sense, but the only people I can see complying with this dictum
are enclosed silent orders of nuns and monks. This priest was
new to the parish and one of his first duties was to officiate at a
funeral. He had never known the deceased; so when he stood in
the pulpit to deliver the homily he was stuck for words. He asked
the congregation if anyone would like to say a few word about
poor John. He was greeted with silence. 'Have none of you got
a good word to say about John?'

A lone voice from the back of the church muttered: 'Well, he
wasn't as bad as his brother.' The only solution I can see to com-
ply with these three dictums is if we were all born blind, deaf
and dumb and then the world would be a great place.

Mike Mahon

Winner All Right

F rancie McGonigle sat at his usual place in the bar of
O'Leary's Pub, purveyor of fine wines and spirits. It was
early afternoon; the place was empty. A copy of the 'Racing
Times' lay on the counter before him. He glanced at his watch
for the fortieth time. Nearly three thirty. Shouldn't be too long
now. He raised the glass to his lips. The golden liquid slid down
his throat, and he felt the warming glow flow through his veins.
'Ah,' he mused, 'mother's milk.' 'Another Power's Gold Label,'
he called to Eddie, the barman, 'and make it a double.' 'What's
the celebration, Francie? Another winner?' 'That's for me to
know and you to guess. Odds of a hundred to one I got. I hope
to be a rich man by dinner time today.'

He took another sip and smacked his lips in appreciation.
'Now. How to spend the money? For John Paul the guitar he al-
ways wanted. But I must try and get him a quiet one. None of
that loud rap music. Jacinta, a difficult child. Hates people, but
loves animals. A dog, or maybe a pet rabbit. But then I'd be left
to clean up the mess after it. I know. I'll get her a tortoise, a
harmless little animal and practically unbreakable. A nice red
dress for the wife. She loves red even though she's colour blind.'

He was rudely woken from his reverie by the loud jangle of
his mobile. Frantically, he thumbed the answer button and
jammed the phone to his ear. 'Dammit, I've managed to switch
the bloody thing off.' He hurriedly keyed in his pin. A metallic
voice answered him. 'That pin number is not recognized. Please
try again.' 'Here, Eddie, give me another drink. A Gold Label. I
need some inspiration. These new-fangled gadgets have me
thwarted.' He sipped the golden liquid. He tried to think. 'The
pin! The pin!' Then it came to him: the wife's birthday. This
time he entered the four digits carefully. The mobile sprang back
to life. 'You have one new voicemail message.' He eagerly

---

pressed play and listened intently. 'Ya boy ya. I've done it. 'Win-
ner All Right.' One thousand smackaroos. She's a darling girl. I
knew she could do it.' He hastily lowered his drink and headed
for the door. 'Here, Francie,' the barman called after him, 'aren't
you even going to give me the name of the horse?' 'Horse? What
horse? It's the wife. She's just had twins and I had a tenner on
at a hundred to one. I remember well the night it all started. It's
not called Powers for nothing, you know. Keep me a case of that
Gold Label.'

Mike Mahon

The Prodigal Son

M avis McGonnigle was in the throes of seventh heaven. The reason for her ecstasy, her youngest and dearest son was returning home after ten years on the missions.

'Gerald my son, the priest,' as she always spoke of him to anyone deranged enough to listen to her, 'has been in darkest Africa among all those heathens and this is his first holiday home.' She had pestered the local Bishop to have him canonised, and only relented in her request when the poor man agreed to have a pew in the local church dedicated to: Fr Gerald Mc Gonnigle, saviour of heathen souls.

Oh, what an occasion; Mavis had been preparing for months. The small terraced house had been spring cleaned twice. Indeed would have been redecorated only for lack of funds. The garden, a riot of flowers, mainly lilies, which Mavis considered the most religious of flowers for such an auspicious occasion.

Her friends had all been invited, but most declined quoting the imminent death of a close relative or some other imaginary family crises. The best dinner service had been rescued from the china cabinet, the family silver, comprising one silver teapot, and a set of cutlery courtesy of The Grand Hotel, polished till it gleamed. She fussed around the house every day, hoovered incessantly and took valium to help herself calm down. She had compelled the whole family to attend and put them under strict orders to be at their best behavior. 'I'll have none of your smart remarks about The Holy Catholic Church, and Sylyia, please wear a skirt that at least covers your knees and keep your er.... appendages under control. Seamus go easy on the drink; last time you almost drove home with the wrong children. Oh, and speaking of children can you all please impress on them the solemnity of the occasion when they, no doubt, will get Father Gerald's blessing.' She had perused for months her collection of cookery books for a feast suitable for a servant of God; fish and a goodly supply of freshly baked loaves.

Finally, the great day arrived. The family were gathered and duly subdued with a liberal sprinkling of Lourdes water, which Mavis frequently topped up from the church font. Sylvia was modestly dressed; the children cowed and Shamus moodily sipping a glass of tonic water. The phone rang. 'Oh, glory be to God , that must be him. He said he'd ring from the airport.''Hello, my darling, how are you? No, no, don't explain; just get a taxi. You've got a friend with you? Great. Bring him too. See you soon.''That was him, Gerald, my son, the priest. He's on his way. Oh my God, I need another valium! Well, maybe I'll have a wee drop of sherry to steady the nerves.' Mavis was flushed and her eyes glowed with excitement. Finally the door bell rang. 'That's him, that's him. Seamus, go pay the taxi. I'm sure Gerald has only pesetas, or what ever money they use in Africa.'

Gerald stood before her, looking healthy and tanned in his clerical garb. 'Mom, it's great too see you. Great to see all of you. I'd like you to meet M'beke.''But, but, he's black!' Mavis blurted out; then realised what she'd said. Her hand flew to her mouth in embarrassment. 'Oh, I am sorry, Mr. M'beke. Please come in; you are very welcome. 'M'beke, smiled indulgently, shook Mavis by the hand. 'Mrs. McGonnigle, how pleased I am to meet you. I'm sure we'll be great friends. May I call you Mom?' Poor Mavis gasped to regain her composure. But of course you may.'

Gerald grasped the moment. 'Mother, I've something to tell you. M'beke and I are partners, we........''Oh, how wonderful. Brothers in Christ. Spreading the word of God together. I'm so happy and proud.' 'Well, not exactly,

Mom. You see we're partners, eh, more in the Biblical sense. We're lovers and plan to get married.'

Mavis Mc Gonnigle never recovered and spent the rest of her days in a Home for the Bewildered. Often she was seen wandering the empty corridors at night, muttering to herself,

'My son, my son. Geraldine, Oh, Geraldine, the fairy.'

Mike Mahon

Gas Meters

W ho could believe that this is a true story, only with changed names of persons and places? Many years ago there lived a young couple named Jack and Jill and their children on the outskirts of a large town. Their home was supplied by town-gas, with the meter being read every two months and a follow-up bill sent by the gas company. Everything was fine until one sunny June morning, when a boy on a bicycle read the gas-meter and triggered the chain of strange events to be described below.

The typical bill would be some two to four pounds, making roughly twenty pounds for the full year. Following the visit of the boy on the bicycle, the bill received was six hundred and seventy two pounds plus some shillings and pence. At going prices, this would cover gas costs over more than thirty years. There was definitely something seriously wrong!

The wife Jill called on her man to research the problem, starting with the gas-meter itself. In the old days, boys on bicycles were required to do hard work in earning their living. That may explain why gas-meters were hidden away in dark dusty holes under stairs, as far back from light and air as possible. Her husband Jack after strenuous efforts emerged sneezing from the glory-hole, but bearing in triumph an un-attached gas-meter. Simple calculation linked this with the daft amount on the bill. It was an old meter, taken out of service some time earlier when a new meter was installed, but read by the boy on that fateful June morning.

Some follow-up action now proved possible. The clerks who sent the bill for six hundred and seventy two pounds could be confronted by the facts. Visiting their office at the gas company, Jack was surprised by their reaction. The amount on the bill was defended as valid. Only after a heated argument was it agreed that this bill be ignored, and the next bill cover the previous two periods. As for taking away the old unattached meter, so as to avoid future mistakes, this was no concern of theirs. All meter fitting and removal was done by a servicing firm located in an-other town. Jack at this point heard a faint but clear cracking sound within his mind. This last straw had broken the back of a camel that lived somewhere deep inside!

With no regrets or apologies available from the gas company clerks, nor any admission of mistake, Jack saw clearly the final necessary act. Justice must be done. He secured the old gas-met-er on the carrier of his bike, and a little later on a sunny July morning carried it into the gas company office. He placed it on the desk of the most aggressive clerk of his last visit with the words: 'This belongs to you.' Jack could see that the man was be-coming rather angry, as he turned away and headed out. But the joy swelling up inside made him break into song as he stepped out onto the sunlit street. No other song but 'I did it my way!'

Eamon Henry

Piano Lesson

J o brought home the good news to her husband Jim - a piano in good condition available at no cost, only take it away - thanks to a notice in the window of the fish and chip shop. For their daughters aged six and nine, they agreed that learning the piano would be very nice indeed. All they needed to arrange for was a van to move the piano from A to B.

However, better have a look at it first, where it resided, at number 7 Woodbine Close. As Jim reached number 7, a fly-past of cawing rooks on his left-hand side portended bad news, if Jim were an ancient Roman, but he wasn't. He found that the man and woman who lived there were out, and didn't have a telephone. Their teenage daughter could offer little help, and so piano discussion proved difficult. At all events, a time of collection for transport was agreed.

Jim found himself admiring the strength and skill of the four van-men, as they manoeuvered that large and heavy object through the living-room door towards a gentle rest beside the fire-place. Next necessity was to get the piano tuned before the girls would start any practice. The report on this was unexpected. Rusty string-wires could of course be replaced but the widespread woodworm could spread quite rapidly throughout the whole house.

Most people do not want their neighbours to think of them as being stupid. Jim and Jo were like that. To solve the problem, the piano must be brought out the back in the dead of night and burned, without any comment or discussion. What can a couple do in this situation, without involving other humans?

Jim took a handsaw and sawed the piano down the middle into two equal halves. He noticed how the saw-teeth made a higher sound while sawing through brass screws than while sawing through the wood. By lifting and pulling, Jo and he managed to move the piano halves out of doors and well away from the house, into the vegetable garden patch, now idle in mid-winter.

By midnight a merry cremation blaze engulfed the piano, whose wood flamed and sparkled. Through the glowing embers there gradually appeared a large iron harp. Jim felt behind and above him the shade of Tom Moore, who spoke clearly through his mind 'Dear harp of my country, in darkness I found thee. Thy breaking heart sounds a final elegy' and, indeed, in the strong heat, the wire chords burst asunder, sounding high, middle and low notes in a final wild threnody.

Such a noble harp deserved a decent burial. In the soft well-worked soil, a shovel could easily provide a suitable grave. As Jim shovelled out the soil onto one side of the hole, he spoke softly some words from Charles Wolfe's poem 'The burial of Sir John Moore' as a suitable burial service. 'We buried him darkly at dead of night, the sods with our bayonets turning' and thus, beneath a Yorkshire vegetable garden, that harp awaits its resurrection.

As they moved back indoors, Jo could feel that Jim was in a thoughtful mood. She fetched the whisky bottle and poured two generous measures. As she handed him one, Jim spoke: 'Life can have its difficult moments.' No reply was needed as they drank in silence.

Eamon Henry

A Woman In His Life

Kay Adams

F reddie Joyce stood in front of the fly-specked mirror above the mantelpiece. He was combing his thinning hair. If he wet it and placed a certain way on his head, he didn't look too bald. Freddie was forty-two years old, tall and spare. He was a quiet man, very shy, especially around the fair sex, which was probably the reason why he still lived at home with his mother. She was sixty-eight years old, a wiry little woman, but she had a spiteful, bitter tongue in her head. If she loved anything or anybody in this world, it was Freddie.

She laughed now, 'Look at ya. Ya think you were goin' to meet the Queen of Sheba, instead of goin' to your sodality meeting. Honestly, Freddie, why don't ya get that bit of fuzz shaved. Ya'd look better for it.' The man's face flushed. He was mortified. 'M...Mother,' he stuttered 'leave me alone. I told you before I'm never going to the barbers again. I like my hair as it is.' After giving it a last pat into place, he started to put on his overcoat. Nancy stood up. She wrapped his woollen scarf around his bony neck. 'Ah, sure son you know I'm only codding ya. It's just that it would be easier to manage if you had it shaved off.'

Paddy lived in Dublin in the Corporation flats in Killarney

Street, but he hated the place. He had to pass all his mother's old cronies, as they gossiped outside their hall doors. They called to him as he passed, 'Hi'ya Freddie, does your mother know you're out?' Always the same joke, the same banter. Smiling at the women, he was glad to escape into the street. When he got outside, he started to breathe freely, away from the stifling presence of his mother. He walked jauntily along, whistling softly. He felt elated. Maybe there might be a few girls in the hall after Sodality. Freddie helped Father Trimble to clean up the church; then they both went into the community hall. It was packed. People were lining up on the floor. Music was playing. It was lively. A man and woman were telling the people how to twist and turn. They were the dance teachers. Everybody was learning a new dance.

Freddie stood against the wall until his friend Pat Fagan came over. 'Come on Fred; it's gas. You don't have to dance with anyone. ' He knew that might get Freddie onto the floor. An hour later, Freddie was laughing heartily. 'Pat,' he gasped, 'I'm knackered; this dance lark is killing me.' The dance teacher turned off the music. Then he said. 'Turn to the person on your left. Put your arm around him or her, whichever way it works out, We are going to teach you how to waltz.' Freddie tried to escape off the floor, but two hands held him in an iron grip. 'No, you don't.' A blonde head just reaching his chest; two merry blue eyes with dark lashes. A pretty girl. It was young Jean Rogers. He knew her from the flats. 'Come on, be my partner,' she pleaded. Freddie was stuck to the floor with shock. 'Are you sure you want me?' He was puzzled. She used to pass him on the staircase as if he didn't exist. 'Yea, come on Freddie.' They stayed dancing together for the rest of the night.

Jean's friends were all paired with fellas, so it seemed natural to her to link Freddie and walk home with him. He was delighted; to have a girl to walk beside him was wonderful, even if it was only for a night. The two people were talking nine to the dozen. Jean liked the man. So what if he was older than her; at least she didn't have to fight him off in the passion stakes. Freddie was a proper gentleman. He listened to Jean as if he was really interested in her. 'Will we go to the chipper?' Freddie didn't want to go home. Jean nodded, 'Yea, I'd love a single.' When they went into Marios all the crowd from the hall were there. 'Get up there Freddie.' The jeers from the young people made him blush, but Jean turned on them. 'Shut up, ya load of gougers. Yiz are only jealous. Freddie is better than any of yiz.' Jean left him at the end of the staircase. Quickly she kissed him on the lips; but before he could say anything she was gone.

He was ecstatic; she must like me. He lay in bed, his heart pounding. This must be love. A feeling he hadn't felt for years crept over him. He couldn't sleep. Then he heard his mother cough in the next room and the feeling vanished. He pushed his knees into his chest, hugging himself as he fell asleep. The next evening when he came home from work his mother was sitting at the fire. No greeting passed her lips. Freddie knew somebody had spilled the beans about him being with a girl. 'What's for dinner, Ma?' Freddie decided to play it cool. 'Your dinner is in the pot,' was the sharp reply. She sat staring into the fire. A coddle was bubbling on the gas. He hated coddle but he didn't say a word. He got a plate and he heaped the sausages, potatoes and gravy onto it. 'Do you want any?' He looked at the still figure. 'No. I don't feel like eating tonight.' The man could hear his anger building. What did he do, only walk a girl home? Where was the sin in that?

The silence in the room grew. Fear was uppermost in

Nancy's mind, fear of loneliness, fear of having no man to protect her. If only she had voiced her fears to him, all would have been well, but she kept silent until Freddie could stand it no longer. 'Ma,' he burst out, 'I'm a grown man. I need a woman in my life. I need to love and be loved. I want a child.' His voice was shaking. He was close to tears. Why couldn't she understand? Nancy nodded her head. 'Well there's plenty of lassies looking for a good catch. You won't have any trouble finding one. But you can forget love. You're too old. All the ones around here are looking for a meal ticket to get outta the flats. Believe me, if you go with someone around here you'll rue the day.' 'Well mother,' Freddie stood up. 'I've been your meal ticket for long enough.'

Nancy couldn't believe it. Freddie standing up to her. 'Ya young cur.' She took a dishcloth and hit him on the side of the head. His carefully constructed hair stood on end. He put on his overcoat and ran out the door. Going downstairs, he bumped into Jean. She was with a fella about her own age. Freddie caught her arm. 'Jean,' he murmured. She was startled. Then she laughed. 'Jaysus Freddie, your bleeding hair is waving goodbye to ya.' The young man she was with said: 'Come on, we're late. Who's that madman?' Freddie had run onto the street, frantic now that he didn't even have a comb to settle himself.

It was very late when he let himself back into his home. Going into his bedroom, he sat on the side of the bed. He looked at the holy picture on the wall. It was the Virgin Mary with her baby Jesus in her arms. His voice filled with emotion, he muttered: 'Was there a day when your son hated you?'

Kay Adams

A Woman Like That

Billy sat in the public house. He was waiting for Flo, his wife. She had gone shopping in the local supermarket. 'Jesus,' he thought. 'I'm sick of this charade every week. She's making a right molly out of me.' Billy was sixty-six years old; he looked much older. Years of plying his trade on the building sites around Dublin had taken its toll. He was a bricklayer by trade, retired now. He was crippled with rheumatism; he had to lean on a stick to help him walk.

Flo rushed into the pub, the plastic bags weighing her down, her face flushed from the exertion. 'I'm gasping for a fag,' she groaned, sitting beside Billy. Smoke drifted into his eyes. 'For God's sake will ya sit away from me; you're choking me with that smoke.' She sat on the other side of the table. 'Nothin' about it when you smoked forty a day until you got frightened of gettin' cancer,' she laughed. 'Your gettin' to be a real oul grouch, so shut up and get me a vodka and white.'

Joe, the barman, smiled at the antics of the old couple. They sat in the same seats every Thursday. In the quiet of the after-noon the trade was slow, so he was often entertained to the two of them arguing.

'What did ya get for dinner?' 'A nice piece of tripe' was the reply. 'Tripe,' Billy roared, 'tripe!!, Could ya not get a man a nice bit of steak and onions?' 'Ya can't chew steak with no teeth and tripe is better for your stomach.' Billy looked at his wife; forty years they were married. 'Ya know you're a cunning bitch. I'll give ya that. Ya turn the tables on me all the time.'

Flo finished her drink. 'Come on. It's time to go home.' 'I'm not goin',' Billy answered. 'I only had two pints. I always have four today.' But his wife was tired. 'Ah Billy, come on,' she coaxed, 'I don't feel very well, let's go.' 'No I'm not goin'.' She knew it was useless arguing with him, he was so stubborn. 'Well

I'm off.' She picked up the keys and started to leave. Billy was in a panic. If she left, he couldn't drink much more; how would he get home? 'Ah come on Flo, have another vodka.' But his wife had walked out the door. He looked over at Joe, 'Another pint there man; sure have one yourself.' Joe shook his head. 'It's too early for me, old man.' 'Old man? Who are you callin' an old man?' Suddenly Billy tried to stand up, but he couldn't get his feet under him.

He drank his pint quietly, watching the door, waiting for Flo to come back, but the shadows of evening were making the pub a very silent lonely place. Billy suddenly felt he wanted to be at home with his wife. He walked out into the street, leaning heavily on a walking stick. He felt frustrated. Why were women so obstinate? He'd never understand them. Flo was such a quiet girl before he met her; but since he retired from work they seemed to argue all the time. In the distance he could see Flo walking slowly towards him. She had her head lowered; so she did not see him. He hurried back to the pub. 'Give us a pint.' Joe was surprised but he didn't pass a remark. Billy sat back in the seat. He was delighted. He could see her face pressed up against the window looking for him. She looked very pale as she sat beside him. 'Have a vodka,' he said quietly. 'You're an old get,' she burst out. 'You know you can't walk home after four pints. I was afraid you might fall.'

It was later on that night. An ambulance with flashing lights screamed through the streets. Flo tried to sit up. 'Billy, where are you?' 'Rest now.' The ambulance man pushed her gently back on to the pillow, 'Billy will be here soon.' 'A massive heart attack,' the doctor told the man when he arrived at the hospital. There was nothing anybody could do.

If was a few weeks later. Billy was sitting in the pub. 'She should have said something.' Guilt gnawed away at him. He knew she had tried to tell him she was sick, but he was too selfish to listen to her. Tears splashed on his hands. Suddenly he felt his heart was breaking. Joe came around the bar. He held the old man. 'Now, now, don't; take it easy, there's a good man.'

Billy sat for a long time in the pub, but he only had two pints. He knew four was out of the question now. But the funny thing was he didn't want any more, there was no kick to it now. Nobody cared if he drank himself to death. 'You know you were an awful pain in the arse Flo all the same,' he chuckled on his way home.

Kay Adams

Poems

The Yellow Stork

Eamon Henry

A sad day's work, oh yellow stork! Your poor shanks stretched after all the crack!

Not for food, I think, but through want of drink, are you lying flattened upon your back!

Great Troy destroyed makes me less annoyed, than your corpse laid out on the stone's bare top.

Not a harm you brought, no deception wrought, you deserve good wine, not bog-hole slop!

My handsome scout, the heart goes out to your quiet head laid at my feet!

How often I have heard your cry, while you drank your fill in the marshy peat!

I Charles your friend will meet my end, from the drink, they say, let them think the worst!

It will not be so, but like gallant crow, that lately died of excessive thirst!

Oh stork so young, my heart is stung, to see you there among the whins!

The rats will stay at your wake all day, and it won't be nice, when the sport begins!

I am quite put out that you didn't shout, that the times were bad, that your strength did fail.

The ice I'd break on Vasey's lake, you could have your fill of Adam's ale!

My sad lament does not extend to blackbird, crane, or song-thrush fair.

Of my stork I sing, great-hearted thing! Like me in his thirst and his yellow hair!

His life he spent on drink intent. For myself betimes there's the day or night

When each dram supplied goes down inside lest I die of thirst, a fearful plight!

The wife has said I'll soon be dead unless I change my tipsy ways.

My blunt reply: she speaks a lie, for the drink will rather prolong my days.

Our stork, you note, had a well-oiled throat, yet he died last night of drought profound!

So, good friends, don't fret! Keep the wind-pipe wet! For no drop ye'll get in the graveyard ground!

Translated from the Irish by Eamon Henry. The original Irish poem is "An Bunnan Buidhe" by author Cathal Buidhe Mac Giollagunna (born circa 1690), as published in FION NA FILIOCHTA (Educational Company of Ireland, 1954 edition, pp. 155-156).

Eamon Henry

Your Hands

A vigil without tears we kept,
And hugged you at Arrivals.
Your knuckles white on trolley bar,
You pushed your wiry frame beside us.
But clenched blue lips gave the game away -
Only stubborness had saved you.
Headstrong,
Bodyweak boy.

Your defiant scrawl
Signed you out
From lonely Toronto Coronary Care.
Pilate medics washed their hands :
'Endo-carditus - travel is dangerous.'
'Tri-cuspid atresia - it's never easy.'
Scalpel words you'd never use.

Dublin Airport to Vincent's Hospital.
To friends you trust at last.
Quiet, asleep.
A mask to breathe.
Fettered by tubes, your hands lie strangely still,
Club-tipped fingers tinged with blue.

Rampant cuticles cover nails.
All tell tales
Of your brave heart,
Fighting from birth
With a hole punched through.
Nature's balance
For a baby blue

All your life you've pumped your golden heart
To fire the power that touched our soul.
And tossed out love for all to catch
And get it back again and more.
You never spared your hands that danced in chat
And wave and clap and slap on back.

You're well again and bound for Oz.
In departure lounge with farewell crowd
Your eyes are smiling as you hug
And hug with talking hands
That joke away our lurking pain.
Your stubborn spirit soars to greet a waiting world.
But we can see those self-same knuckles whiten
As - unfelt - they tighten
On your bag
...... and we pray.

Rick Quinn

London Underground

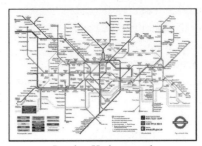

London Underground

A dark tunnel mouth to my left, a bend to the right
And where I stood in the middle - light.
The power line prominent between the tracks.
Two figures near me, one young, tall, lithe with a briefcase,
The other, struggling with crutches, legs bent, back twisted.
The sign read 'Train in 3 minutes, London Underground.'
The man with crutches strained to make his way along the plat-
form.
I looked at the tall young man. He looked at me.
The sign read 'Train in 2 minutes, London Underground.'
The man with crutches moved to the platform's edge, his back to-
wards us.
The power line seemed more ominous. 'Too close, too close,'
I thought.
He swayed and swerved, his crutches rising overhead.
Back and forth they waved till one dropped from his grasp.
The sign read 'Train in 1 minute, London Underground.'
'I'll mind your briefcase.' I had read the young man's thoughts.
That was all I could do.
He dashed and hooked his arms under the shoulders of the sway-
ing man.
He grappled and fought to restrain that helpless writhing weight.

The headlights shone from the bend.
The train non-stopping hurtled through - a stillness in its wake.
An attendant with an invalid chair appeared.
The disabled man was wheeled away.
I looked at the tall young man. He looked at me.
I returned his briefcase.
That was all I could do.

Opal Peard

We Arise Today

Patrick's cry glides across the centuries
To our land every spring-March day
Facing the future with joy and celebration
We are happy to hear it yet again

We arise today

Gathering on sidewalks in towns and villages
To savour the evergreen remembrances
Of the slave-man saint from afar
Who came to walk and live amongst us

We arise today

Through hardships famine and grievous loss
Heartbreak sorrow and lonely empty homes
Through recession job-losses and family unrest
Through sickness poverty and even despair

We arise today

Ancestor lineage of staunch generations
Shows a nation of pride, purpose and place
On Atlantic's edge of wild sea foam
Standing bravely facing elements of uncertainty

We arise today

Now Patrick's cry is again heard in 21st century
Across a glorious fertile land – our salvation
His green-leaf trinity forever raised on high
A nation bows in humility - gratitude to our Redeemer

We arise today

Maureen Maloney

May

Gathering lilac in May

I love it when May comes around again
With its smile of promise and its breath of lilac
Warming with a purring feel
Memories locked away all year.
But most of all I come to remember her in May –
My father's maiden sister, Auntie May.

To save on bus fares she cheerfully swung her lame leg
Along the Grand Canal from Lullymore Terrace in Rialto
To McMorrough Road in Terenure.
There to care for us when we lost our Mammy
To a sanatorium shut away for such lonely years.

May, her hair in a bun, her shining face smelling of
Fresh soap that knew no make-up.
With gentle soothing voice she used to quell
Our children's squabbles -
'Birds in a nest must agree' she cooed
And led our prayers.

Untutored she passed on the positive words of her own philo-
sophy.
Did we appreciate her then and did she know we loved her?
Yet years on, grown-up children cried
To see her laid out in Child of Mary robes.
We did not need to be told then that we had a new saint.

When May sun gilds the roads of Terenure and Harold's Cross
I see her leave her heavenly host
To wing her way along the canal
From Lullymore Terrace to McMorrough Road.

Rick Quinn

Longing For The Hills

Barbados gave a sweaty night, between the showers of rain.
The throbbing drums of vans from slums did cause his ears to pain.
The chirping frogs with barking dogs had joined in loud affray.
They'd keep it up without a stop until the break of day.

He rubbed his arms with soothing cream, to try and stop the itch,
And spray-gunned a mosquito, to kill blood-sucking bitch,
While beetles all, both great and small, climbed up and down and flew,
He laced a shot of rum with juice to boost his strength anew.

There are cool days and quiet nights without the sweat and noise,
And these indeed could come again as deeply valued joys.
The bracing air of Dublin hills refresh his aging blood,
Like throbbing cry of kestrel's young tree-hopping through the
wood.

Like hare and deer and whirring grouse and all the things that move
Among the heather, and the woods upon the hills above.
He misses them, but hopes indeed to find them all once more
Where they will be, when he has passed – a happy thought to store!

Eamon Henry

Mountain Conquered

That bleakness, that unending cold,
The harshness of the sky,
The ice, the glistening ice,
A sadness all foretold.

No soft outline,
No gentle face,
Relentless, hard, with deep ravine,
Blizzard, blindness and crevasse.

No air to breathe
Not fleet of foot,
No beauty, no relief,
Hardship, solitude and loss.

But you have reached your goal,
You have won your way,
You obeyed the inner force,
Uncovered, cold, you lie.

We carry on where you left off.
We fulfil your dreams.
We who stayed at home,
Ours are the aching hearts.
Ours the loneliness .

Opal Peard

Anthony

You on the top landing, I in a panic.
You about to tumble down the old brown stairs.

With glazed stare you swayed,
On the top steps under the leaky beam.

Just in time, I caught your little hunched shoulders.
Guided you back to bed, screamed for my mother.

Then Doctor Burke came. A neighbour's phone!
No bottle cure today, only a medic's frown.

Screeching tyres, ambulance din, thunderous knock
And hurrying feet on the old brown stairs.

Wrapped up in grey blanket you were carried away
My five year old brother, down the old brown stairs.

From around the corner at Cork Street Fever Hospital,
The dread news came, Bacterial Meningitis!

Now older than my eleven years. How I cried for you.
In your little white coffin. Already an angel!

We have cemented your memory, Rosemarie and I.
We christened our first son, Anthony.

Paddy Conneff

Curlews

Curlews calling on the strand: Conroy, Conroy riabhach!
Young brindled Conroy, member of their tribe, got lost somehow.
Their search for him goes on, yes, even now!

The curlews know it all, indeed they do!
Tide coming and tide going, and at full tide
The little fields among the uplands, too.

Curlews crying on the strand, running beside the tidal streams,
Are they crying also for my own lost youthful dreams?
Conroy, Conroy, riabhach!

Eamon Henry

Give Us Back Our Medical Cards

A quiet day at Leinster House

From the Alexander Hotel we overflow

Into St Andrew's Church in Westland Row

On crutches and sticks we march on the pews

A new silver army in ones and twos

Our voices angry in this holy place

Remind our leaders we're a rebel race

Brian Cowen's man drowned by the old folks' shout

'We don't want to hear you – out,out,out,out!'

'We shall overcome', sings a man from Clare

While like him our hands wave high in the air

With our smiles and tears we greet his brave boom

A little bit of heaven in the doom and the gloom

The Wednesday protesters pack Molesworth Street

While from a blue truck the speakers entreat:

'O show them respect, they helped build this land'

Waves of anger crash on Leinster House strand.

Posters bristle with advice for the Dail:

'Why don't they just shoot us', one asks them all.

Shoulder to shoulder we clap and we cheer

Our medical cards just can't disappear

> *'Give a thing and take it back*
>
> *God will ask you where's that*
>
> *You'll say you don't know*
>
> *God will send you down below'*

Camaderie from Ardee to Macroom

A little bit of heaven through the doom and the gloom.

Rick Quinn

In Praise Of Volunteering

Pauline o'Regan
Manager St. Bridget's Resource Centre

It's a feel good thing, I've much to contribute.

Even if only newsletters to distribute

The laughter, the tears, the endless chatter,

Having fun spending time with people who matter

I'm not on the scrapheap, up there sitting

It sure beats lonely, at home with my knitting.

There is poker and scrabble, and outings galore

There is friendship and kindness, who could want more.

I'm making a difference of that there is no doubt

I've learned skills unheard of, and more coming out.

I'm often tired and weary, but oh, what the heck,

I'm still alive, and I always had a sore back.

I'm not sitting at home waiting for my maker to call.

I'm out there, living the life, having a ball.

So here's to our Volunteers, happy and true

To your calling and giving the good that you do

You are special, you're chosen, you're wonderful too.

Killester and the world needs people like you.

Pauline O' Regan

Memories

I remember my youth, oh happy times,

Soft summer days when the sun always shines

Laughter and fun like nobody's child

Climbing trees, bloody knees, breaking hearts, running wild

The smell of the morning before the world was awake

To hear the dawn chorus, down by the lake,

The bark of the fox in the valley below

Were Granny's hens still safe, we will soon know

The hedgerows abundantly gave of their treasure,

Watercress, hazelnuts, blackberries in full measure

Raiding neighbours' orchards for apples and plums

If the gardener caught us we went home with sore bums

We'd meet by the river in our own special place

Stepping stones, rushing water, oh what a race.

Sometimes we got soaked, but that's half the fun,

We'd 'borrow' a boat, if the salmon was on a run.

The harvest time with the barns full of corn

The dance for the workers went on until morn

The bittersweet time when our free days were numbered

Back to school we went, oh how we grumbled.

Memories are there innocent though they be

When the world for a child was a safe place to be

Greatest concern, would my pony win the race?

At the field day with my friends I'd be happy with a place.

Weather turns cold, hunting season begins.

Gallops thru the fields, the hunting horn dins.

Yapping of the hounds turns to fever pitch,

Next thing you know you end up in the ditch.

I'm back there again but only in dreams,

When days were filled with adventures and schemes

Could we be there again, would the magic return?

Would we still catch a trout, between the rocks in the burn?

Where no tree was too high, no river too deep

We swam with the fishes, went home only to sleep.

My friends are all scattered all over the world,

Some gone to their rest, their life's story untold.

But it's nice to remember, to cherish that time.

Was'nt life wonderful and the memories are mine.

Pauline O'Regan

Biographies

AMONG OUR CONTRIBUTORS:

BRIAN BREATHNACH
Was born in Dublin in 1958 and attended De La Salle College Churchtown and Rockwell College Co. Tipperary. He spent one year at the National College of Art and Design Dublin in the mid 1970's. From 1982 Breathnach lived in Paris intermittently for three years where he worked as an artist's assistant for the Irish painter Michael Farrell at 'La Ruche' and began exhibiting his work professionally. In 1986 Breathnach moved to the Algarve coast of Portugal where he continued to exhibit his paintings and work as a portrait artist. In 1987 he carried out a portrait of the German writer Gunter Grass when they met in the Algarve and he made a return visit to Paris to meet with the Irish writer Samuel Beckett and make his portrait. In 1989 Breathnach returned to Dublin where he continues to live and work as a painter and portrait artist.

PADDY CONNEFF
Was born in the outer Liberties of Dublin in 1936. He went to school at Synge Street CBS and Bolton Street College of Technology. He qualified as a Chartered Surveyor and worked in Dublin. He is a life long member of the Dodder Anglers and has served as President. He has also served as President of the Irish Trout Fly Fishing Association, and as Captain of the Irish team in the Four Home Nations International. He fished in all four countries and was twice a member of a victorious Irish team. Paddy was also an athlete, ran the mile for 'Synger' in the Leinster Colleges, and was later a 400 metres hurdler. He is a member of the Ballyroan Writers' Circle.

EAMON HENRY

Born in May 1932, Eamon is a widower with five grown-up children and several grandchildren. Originally from County Sligo, he has spent most of his life in Dublin, working as an statistician/economist at both the Central Statistics Office and the Economic and Social Research Institute. A specialist in the estimation of economic impacts of tourist expenditure, he has published several reports, both for Bórd Failte and for overseas organisations, including researching six Caribbean countries while based at the Caribbean Tourism Organisation in Barbados during 1999-2000. Recently retired, Eamon enjoys spending some of his free time writing short stories and verse.

JOHN LONERGAN

Is a native of County Tipperary and worked in the Irish Prison Service for over 42 years. He was Governor of Mountjoy Prison from 1984 until his retirement in June 2010, with the exception of four years he spent as Governor of Portlaoise, commencing in November 1988.

He believes that real and meaningful change, personal or otherwise, cannot be enforced on people and the challenge is to find the good in others and to nurture it. His philosophy is that the more human beings become aware of their own humanity, the more likely they are to treat others with respect.

JOHN MACNALLY

International singer. His biographical details are contained in his articles.

MIKE MAHON

Born in Dublin and educated at CBS Synge St. Joined the Cadet School in the Curragh after leaving school. Left there to take up commercial flying. Did aerial photography in Ireland, North and South. Joined various airlines and worked in Nigeria, Bahrain, U.K., Holland, France, Belgium and finally back to Aer Lingus. Did a BA in my 'spare time' with Open University. I have two daughters, Lisa and Aoife and a son Michael. I am now retired and would to try my hand at some creative writing.

Joined a writing group in a local library and am involved in writing projects with the Terenure Enterprise Centre.

IAN O'DOHERTY

Ian is an Irish journalist, and TV contributor best known for his daily column 'iSpy' in the Irish Independent. Known for his wry wit and opinionated take on life, his daily dose of commentary on Ireland and beyond has become an additive must read for Irish mornings.

AIDAN O'HARA

Donegal-born Aidan is a prize-winning author and broadcaster. Has worked as a presenter and producer with RTÉ and CBC and now writes full-time. His writings include a biography of Delia Murphy, *I'll live 'til I die - the story of Delia Murphy*, published 1997, and his story of the Irish in Newfoundland, *Na Gaeil i dTalamh an Éisc*, published in 1998. It won the *Oireachtas '97* literary award for a work in prose, and was nominated for The Irish Times Literature Prize in 1999. His essay, 'Judge Charles Patrick Daly (1816-99)' is due for publication in 2011 in *Irish Soldiers, American Wars* (Irish Academic Press), editors Dr. David Noel Doyle and Dr. Arthur Mitchell. His 'Come, pack up your

Store...' Emigration from County Longford in the 19th and 20th centuries, was published in December 2010 in *Longford – History and Society* (Geography Publications). He writes regularly for several journals and magazines as a book reviewer and writer on historical subjects.

MAUREEN MALONEY

Born in Holles Street, Dublin, of Mayo parents. Loved writing short stories and poems since her teens. Had a few articles published in local papers, one as a lament on the death of a friend and another on a *Day at the Races*. Has been a member of the AITS writers since the beginning. It would be her dream to have something of hers broadcast on *Sunday Miscellany*.

OPAL PEARD

Opal was born in Dublin and has lived most of her life in the suburbs. She has attended all the sessions of a Creative Writing Group which was set up in the Terenure Enterprise Centre in 2010 under the guidance of Rick Quinn. She is married to Noel and is the mother of two sons and a daughter and a grandmother of one grandson and five granddaughters. Some of her written work is on display in the Enterprise Centre.

RICK QUINN

Rick studied science at UCD but always wanted to write. He followed a career in training and in IT in the UK and Ireland. When he took early retirement as an IS manager with a major Irish company in the 90's, he returned to his first love – writing; he had been writing short stories and poetry in his spare time for years. His poem '*Your Hands*', included in this collection, won an award in a poetry competition. Rick has written for the *Aware* magazine and was its editor for several years.

In 2010 he facilitated a Bealtaine project in the Terenure Enter-prise Centre, which involved members of the Active IT Society writing their memoirs. When this proved a success he was invited to conduct a number of creative writing courses in the Terenure Enterprise Centre and in St Brigid's Resource Centre in Killester.

The other contributors speak for themselves in their memoirs.